What Matters

MARY KENNEDY

What Matters

Reflections on Important Things in Life

HACHETTE
BOOKS
IRELAND

First published in 2015 by Hachette Books Ireland

A CIP catalogue record for this title is available from the British Library.

ISBN 978 1 473 62170 1

Typeset in Goudy Old Style by Bookends Publishing Services.
Printed and bound in Great Britain by Clays Ltd, St Ives plc.

Hachette Books Ireland's policy is to use papers that are natural, renewable and recyclable products and made from wood grown in sustainable forests. The logging and manufacturing processes are expected to conform to the environmental regulations of the country of origin.

Hachette Books Ireland
8 Castlecourt Centre
Castleknock
Dublin 15, Ireland

A division of Hachette UK Ltd
Carmelite House
50 Victoria Embankment
London EC4Y 0DZ

www.hachette.ie

For Eva and Benny on their engagement,
wishing them lots of happiness.

Contents

*'The scariest moment is always
just before you start.'*

Stephen King

1.

Nothing to It!

*'There is nothing to writing.
All you do is sit down at a typewriter and bleed.'*

Ernest Hemingway

And so, as I reach another milestone in life by turning sixty, I take my seat at the laptop once again and embark on a further chronicle of all the joys and sadnesses, the good and the not so good aspects of this mortal coil that have made me what I am. I know from talking to people as I travel the country for *Nationwide* that I am not unique. The things that make me happy and sad, the things that matter to me, are also the things that matter to most people: relationships, family, friends, home, health, work. It is my earnest wish that the people who read the stories that unfold between the covers of this book will feel consoled, inspired and, above all, comforted by the fact that we all strive to do our best in life, and in work, and aim to knock a lot of fun out of it as we travel the road together.

Ernest Hemingway has a point, you know. The hardest part of this exercise is the physical act of sitting down at the writing machine, in my case a laptop – I do type using the correct fingers, having learned that skill in secondary school under the tutelage of Sister Bernadette, a kind, saintly woman who deserved better than a bunch of giddy teenagers sitting behind a row of typewriters at the end of a long school day. She never allowed us to refer to the skill as 'typing'. No abbreviations for her. It was not a class that we took too seriously, I regret to say as there were no exams at the end of it. We were philistines. The only classes to which we gave our full attention were the ones that would be examined. I am very grateful to Sister Bernadette now for her perseverance because it is very satisfying to type using all my fingers in the right places.

I enjoy the physical act of pressing the keys. I wonder will I still feel the same way when I'm halfway through this book and want to get away from the laptop and the 'typewriting'!

The late, great Irishwoman and author Maeve Binchy shared Hemingway's view of writing. I heard her taking questions from an audience following a talk she'd given on creative writing. Her answer to the query about the most difficult aspect of writing was short and pithy:

> *'The hardest part is sitting down at the computer and pressing the On button.'*

Great minds think alike, obviously. Hemingway's reference to bleeding is a bit off-putting, admittedly, but I know what he means. There will be days when the juices will flow and the words will gallop out of my heart and onto the page, and there will be days when it will be like pulling teeth or getting blood from a stone. That will not be pleasant. I will persevere, though, because I want to do this. I am grateful that I have been invited, for a fourth time now, to write a book. I appreciate that there are many people who love to write and find it hard to get their work published. They have a passion for writing, for telling their story, that is undiminished by the difficulties of publication. They are undeterred and I hope their perseverance pays off and they get the opportunity to present their work to the public eventually because it is a moment of great satisfaction when the finished product comes through the letterbox and the endless hours spent staring at the screen seem worthwhile all of a sudden.

I am humbled by the reaction I have had to the previous three books that I have written. People come up to me and say they related to something I wrote – they went through the same turmoil or adventure. It's nice to realise we are not alone, that other people feel the same way as we do about things, that we all have our struggles and our achievements and that we all do our best to live our lives fully and to take encouragement and consolation from each other.

I have established my work station so that when I have a spare minute or a moment of inspiration I can just sit down and write immediately. The way I'm feeling now, at the very start of this adventure, I think 'a spare minute' will be a more likely scenario than the latter 'moment of inspiration'.

I'm at the stage of thinking I have nothing to say. My friends and family would disagree. I am not behind the door when it comes to giving my opinion and I have got to the stage in life where I have to be true to myself. All through life, my default position has been that of a pleaser, which is not always the best way to be - doing things to keep others happy. I was painfully shy as a child. I wouldn't even ask for things in a shop. My mother got fed up of me saying to her, 'Will you ask for me?' when I'd be spending my few bob to buy Christmas presents for the family years ago. And if it was a case of having to return a purchase which didn't fit, for instance, I would die of mortification, blush bright red and want the floor to open and swallow me up. I have moved on from those days but the underlying shyness is still there. Now, I take a deep breath and say what I have to say.

I have dealt with a lot of life's issues in my previous books. I have spoken of the heartbreak of losing my parents and I have been overwhelmed by the number of people who were reminded of their own parents' lives and deaths by reading *Lines I Love*. I have broached the thorny subject of body image and ageing and a lot of women seem to have taken consolation from the fact that we all go through the same dilemmas – trying to hold on to youth and finally coming to terms with the fact that we cannot turn back the clock and that every age has its beauty. This is as good a place as any to give you my favourite quotation about this subject. I included it in *Lines for Living* and if I had a euro for every woman who has said to me that she has adopted it as her mantra, I'd be a wealthy bunny!

'First you are young,
then you are middle aged;
then you are old;
then you are wonderful.'
Lady Diana Cooper

These are the words of Lady Diana Cooper, a member of the British aristocracy, born in 1892 and widely regarded as the most beautiful woman in England when she was young. Obviously her head wasn't turned by this adulation. She acknowledges in those lines that we are the sum of our parts and that it takes a lot more than a

8

pretty face and smooth skin to make a person wonderful and beautiful.

My description of menopause certainly struck a chord in *Lines for Living*. I wrote quite candidly about my experiences and, I have to admit, I was surprised by the number of people who told me I was very brave to do so. Hello? What is all that about? Is menopause something that middle-aged women should only whisper about among themselves? Is it indelicate to talk about it? I have two thoughts on this. First, people who feel it is 'brave' to discuss menopause are often caught up in the delusion that it heralds the end of a woman's allure in the eyes of the opposite sex. A shallow mindset, I think. Second, it's a bonus to go through it because it means you are still alive. I have lost friends before the middle stage of life and it is a heart-rending tragedy for their families and friends. So let's hear it once more for the big M and the symptoms, affectionately referred to as the seven dwarfs of menopause: Itchy, Bitchy, Wrinkly, Sweaty, Sleepy, Bloated, Forgetful.

My workstation is the dining-room table. There will be no meals served in this room for the foreseeable future.

The table is facing the garden so that I can look out through the conservatory and contemplate the trees and the flowers and feel inspired by the beauty of the great outdoors. That's the theory anyway. The weather has been so bad recently that I feel I might be better pulling down the blinds and forgetting that there is an outside. I have a scented candle that I will light whenever I sit here to write. I will push the On button and hope I will not bleed. I will look forward to the process of sharing my thoughts and hoping that they bring a bit of comfort or a smile to the reader.

As I set out on this adventure, one difference I notice from the previous three occasions is that I am enthusiastic about it. Four years ago when I began writing *Lines for Living*, I had to drag myself to the computer on occasion. I would wash floors, clean windows, iron clothes and make unnecessary phone calls rather than sit down on the chair and write. I was not confident that I could write anything of substance that people would want to read. Perhaps that was the effect of the menopause on me. There's no doubt it can gnaw away at your self-confidence and it's only when you come out the other side that you realise what you've been through.

Turning sixty last year was a real watershed for me. I regained a confidence that had been in short supply. This is the first time I have started a book without agonising over what people will make of it, whether they will adopt that who-does-she-think-she-is mentality. I have lived long enough now to be happy in my own skin and in my own life and to realise that we are all in this together and we can support each other in lots of ways.

So it's once more unto the breach for the next while. I will take every opportunity to write. I will take the laptop with me when I travel – I have two trips planned already. They might shed some light on certain aspects of life. That's the joy of travel. It broadens the mind and opens the heart. The twelfth-century Persian poet Rumi, one of my favourites, throws a positive light on this:

'Travel brings power and love back into your life.'

That'll do nicely. I will reflect on things that have happened in the four years since *Lines for Living* was published – the experiences I have had, the people I have met, the happy occasions I have enjoyed and the losses I have endured, and the change in family life as my children have grown up and moved on with their adult lives.

I wrote about the empty nest in my last book. Little did I know that was just the tip of the iceberg. A child leaving home to move in with a friend about five miles away was a huge jolt to my world. I didn't know it then but within twelve months my youngest child, my baby, would move a bit further than five miles away. Off she went to Korea and Australia, leaving a very sad mammy behind. That's a tale worth telling.

I will write honestly, from the heart, about what matters to me in life. Invariably this will revolve around people and relationships, emotions, struggles, challenges, joys, because these are the things that make up the rich tapestry of life for me.

I have been impressed by other people as I have navigated my way through the last four years of life. Their stories will pop up between the covers of this book, I'm sure. I will recount some of the adventures that I have had in recent times and I will look forward, as always, to putting the finishing touches to the work and writing with satisfaction, hopefully, the words 'The End' on the final page.

Another sociable aspect to writing a book is the anticipation of the launch. I have been very lucky and privileged to have had my previous three books launched by people whom I admire, who accepted my invitation to send my efforts out into the big world. Mary Harney launched my memoir, *Paper Tigers*. She was Minister for Health at the time and extremely busy, but she took the time to come along and reminisce about our time in school in Clondalkin. Mary was a year ahead of me in Coláiste Bríde and her future commitment to service could be seen even then when she insisted that we should have the opportunity to study honours Maths. This did not go down too well with the Presentation Sisters, who didn't have the staff to provide honours Maths to us girls and, truth be told, really didn't see the point of it either. Mary put her foot down, however, and insisted it was our right. The problem was solved by allowing girls from the convent to go to Moyle Park, the boys' school, for honours Maths a few times a week. As you can imagine, the class was highly subscribed!

Book number two was *Lines I Love* and Pat Kenny did the honours on that occasion. His mother and mine were friends. Connie Kenny was one of a group of my mother's women friends who would come to our house regularly for tea and sandwiches and cakes and a catch up, occasions on which my mother would pull out all the stops: the fire lit in the good room, china tea set, starched tablecloth and napkins. There was a lovely warm feeling about those evenings. The ladies were always eager to hear how we were getting on and see how big we were getting, and we always looked forward to the following day when we'd get to eat the leftover sandwiches and cream cakes. Pat remembered those days too and it was nice to hear about those gatherings from a different perspective.

Lines for Living was published four years ago and on that occasion Martin McAleese spoke at the launch. He and I have been part of the same walking group for a long time now and we have had good chats as we pounded the paths along the Camino de Santiago de Compostela and on other occasions over the years. He has an encyclopaedic knowledge of GAA and a mischievous sense of humour, so the slagging quite often divides along county lines. He is also incredibly fit so, as well as thinking of a witty answer to his ribbing, you have to keep putting one foot in front of the other at breakneck speed. I love those outings – we have them a few times a year and they are always memorable for the walking.

As well as the Camino de Santiago, we have walked in the footsteps of St Francis of Assisi, followed the paths of Celtic spirituality on the Aran Islands and taken on beautiful mountains and valleys all around Ireland. This year's Camino will see us all gather for four days in the Burren, another gem of the Irish landscape that will remind us of our rich and ancient heritage. The trips are also memorable for the kindness and gentleness of the people who make up the group. They are open, friendly, thoughtful, incredibly loyal people who would bend over backwards to help a friend in need. They are good company and good fun. I enjoy spending time with them and I always return feeling positive and focused about what matters in my life.

At the launch of *Lines for Living*, Martin picked up on some of the themes in the book that show how similar our aspirations are, and I was delighted because that, as I have said before, is one of the joys of writing these books. The fact that somebody realises they are not alone in their fears or anxieties and takes comfort from that realisation makes it worthwhile. Martin made reference to one particular quotation from the book which is a favourite of mine and sums up the basic premise by which I try to live life:

'There is no hope of joy except in human relations.'
Antoine de Saint-Exupéry

I had made up my mind that *Lines for Living* was going to be my final foray into the world of writing. Therefore the launch was followed by a party at my house. I was surprised by a wonderful cake with the cover of the book in icing. Friends gathered and we ate, drank and sang – and I breathed a sigh of relief. Last book finished. Never say never, though. Here we go again. I'm looking forward to looking inside my heart once more and extracting the feelings and the concerns I have at this milestone of my life. I will share the happy moments and the challenges that have come my way and my sincere wish is that those who read them will feel a sense of belonging, with me, to a community that cares for us and wants us to negotiate this life in a meaningful and compassionate way, surrounded by those we love and those who love us.

And so to work.

I had it all planned. It was a Monday, the start of the week, a time of resolution and new beginnings, the perfect time to get started on this new book about what matters to me at this stage of my life. Things didn't quite work out the way I had envisaged.

Monday seemed full of hope and promise as I anticipated it from the safe distance of the weekend. I had a busy enough morning but arrived back at the house at lunchtime with the afternoon clear of everything but the book. I knew what I wanted to start writing about: the female line in my family and the fact that I come from a strong band of resolute, hardworking, determined women. By that Monday lunchtime, though, I reckon those qualities had got diluted on their journey through the generations to me. I'm definitely hardworking but the strength and the resolution and determination come and go. That Monday, they were in short supply. I felt small, confused, indecisive, unsure. I don't remember feeling the extent of that insecurity as deeply as I have in the past few months.

I was always so full of energy and enthusiasm for any and every kind of project. Years ago, when my children were small and in bed, happily asleep, if I didn't have any school work to prepare, I'd embark on a bit of spring cleaning. Sure what else would you be doing at half eight on a Tuesday night, for instance? I remember the great satisfaction of getting up on a chair, dressed for battle in an apron and a pair of rubber gloves, armed with a damp cloth and a ton of Jif to scour the tops of the cupboards. The tops of the cupboards, if you please! That nobody would ever see. I just needed to know they were clean. Why? I really can't answer that question now. It seemed like a good idea at the time.

There was no talk back then of obsessive-compulsive behaviour. In fact, the first introduction any of my peers got to that was Jack Nicholson collecting endless bars of soap and washing his hands every few seconds in *As Good As It Gets*. And we all laughed at the good of it. I know now that my working my way around the kitchen in the evenings instead of relaxing or chatting on the phone or reading a book or watching TV, was just ridiculous and more of a negative reflection on my ability to relax and enjoy life than any badge of domestic honour. For me, reading a book or watching TV was something that could only be justified when all the work was done and that work included cleaning places that would never see the light of day.

The good news is that I stopped that nonsense of cleaning everything that moves and everything that doesn't - though not all that long ago. I still like my house to be tidy and I think a good spring clean is therapeutic after the dark and dusty days of winter. It's nice to go through wardrobes and boxes and cupboards and throw out things that don't owe us anything. I'm left with a light, airy feeling that I value and look forward to, and which sets me up for a good energetic summer ahead.

When I've done the annual sorting of the house, I concentrate on the garden. But I haven't had that light airy burst of energy this year. I feel no different to the way I did all winter because, this year, I haven't tackled the house. And I regret that. My home is my sanctuary and my castle, I suppose, but there are moments when I find it very hard to bother about it. There's a feeling of 'what's the point?', which is very new to me and which

I don't like. I try not to give in to it but sometimes it's overwhelming. I just don't seem able to summon the motivation as easily as I once did.

I've examined my mindset and tried to come up with answers about why this should be the case. What has happened to make me, that person who has always had great regard for homemaking, indifferent in this way? For goodness sake, I'm the mammy who used to get up at an ungodly hour when I was travelling early to some far-off location to film for *Nationwide*. And why did I get up even earlier than I had to? So that I could make fairy cakes that the children would smell as they were getting up and ready for school and college, so that they would have warm, fresh buns for their breakfast. Making memories! The reality is that time has moved on. The college days are over and the children are adults. They don't have their own homes yet but they're definitely moving in that direction. So there's nobody to bake those buns for. And when that enthusiasm wanes, it's hard to maintain it for the other aspects of homemaking like the spring clearout and the garden. I have come to the realisation that I was doing it for others to a large degree and now that those others are otherwise engaged and focused, I am quite definitely less enthusiastic about home. I find it hard to focus on a particular project. I can spend a lot of time vacillating, telling myself I will do it later, but later doesn't always come.

And that brings me right back to that fateful Monday and my determination to start writing a chapter about the womenfolk in my family and the way they have influenced my life – and the procrastination and lack of words written on the subject. It's not that I hadn't thought about it in depth. It had been toing and froing in my conscious and subconscious mind all weekend. I had made notes about significant memories of my grandmother and read again some details of her family tree that my cousin Barry had unearthed and which make for very interesting reading.

On that Monday, though, I just could not get going on that positive track. I lacked focus. I told myself I didn't know where to start. I felt quite insecure and totally lacking in confidence. I read back over a chapter in the last book I'd written, *Lines for Living*, and convinced myself I would never be able to write like I had done four years earlier. I stared at the screen that had one line written on it: 'Woman is the light of God', a lovely quotation from Rumi which you would think would be inspirational as a starting point.

I told myself I was being silly, that I should cop myself on, stop feeling sorry for myself, get on with it. Yet nothing happened.

I know from talking to other women that this is a state of being which afflicts us all, particularly as we get older. You'd think the opposite would be the case, that the maturity and wisdom we have gained as we progressed through life with all its ups and downs would galvanise our spirit and our courage and confidence. Sadly that is not always the case and there are two things worth noting about this: we should not beat ourselves up when the chutzpah is missing, and we should grasp life with both hands when it returns. I have found in recent years that the moments of self-doubt are more frequent but at least I recognise them for what they are now and I won't try to be something I'm not when they rear their ugly little heads. That's what I told myself on that Monday, bloody Monday, anyway.

So I got up from the laptop and got in the car and headed off to the garden centre. In the pouring rain. I ended up looking at outdoor rattan coffee sets that would be perfect in a country that enjoys several months of unbroken sunshine. I don't think I'd get a return on my investment in this country in my lifetime. From that fantasy section of the garden centre, I moved on to the much more affordable plant section and, lo and behold, I came home with a walk-in plastic greenhouse. I do not know how I got to this age and stage of my life without one! Think of the fresh lettuces and radishes that I will be harvesting this summer. Not to mention the growbags that I can fill with tomato plants and courgettes and peppers. The possibilities are endless. Or would be if the greenhouse was a lot bigger than it actually is. It was reduced to half price at twenty euro. It's a bargain! It's also self-assembly. That skill is not one that I have been blessed with. Anytime I have tried it, I've ended up with spare parts – unintentionally! So I will be depending on one of the boys to erect this fine edifice that may have us self-sufficient in salads this summer. Or not.

There's a little voice in my head that's reminding me that you get what you pay for. And twenty euro is not a fortune for a greenhouse. Even if it were full price, forty euro is not a huge amount for a greenhouse either. I'll give it a go, though. And even if it blows over in the first big wind that it encounters it'll have been worth the little bit of a lift it gave me that afternoon, when I was deflated after spending too long telling myself I could do better.

We women are very hard on ourselves sometimes. I hope that by reading this some will realise that we should be a bit more accommodating of our weak days when we lack motivation, when we feel a bit low. We should mind ourselves and mind each other.

For me, at certain times, there's a melancholy that is never too far away, no matter how hard I try to anticipate it and head it off at the pass. And I do try. I keep myself very busy. I visit friends. I make trips. I get in the car and head off. Usually removing myself from the situation lifts the melancholy. There are times, however, when it's there to meet me on my return from the evasion strategy, but that's OK. I can deal with it more easily because I have had a bit of diversion and I remind myself of the words of St Teresa of Ávila:

'Let nothing disturb you,
Let nothing affright you,
All sorrows pass.
God alone remains.
All will be well.'

There's nothing like a night's sleep to change my outlook on life and the world. Tuesday dawned and I woke looking forward to a bright new day and to a feeling of confidence that would enable me to start writing about the wonderful women who went before me and who will come after me and around whose lives I am proud to be entwined.

'A woman is the full circle.
Within her is the power to create,
nurture and transform.'
Diane Mariechild

*'Ah, how quickly the hands on the clock circle
toward the future we thought was far away!
And how soon we become our mothers.'*

Peggy Toney Horton

2.
Mná na hÉireann

'All women become like their mothers.
That is their tragedy.
No man does. That is his.'

Oscar Wilde

I was going to begin this chapter with Rumi's quotation about woman being the light of God but, on mature reflection, I think Oscar Wilde's insight into our relationships with our mothers fits the bill nicely.

If I had a euro for every time I said to myself as a teenager and young woman that I was going to do things differently to my mother – live my life differently, raise my children differently, decorate my house differently – I'd be a rich woman. However, not only have I followed in her footsteps in the way I live my life, I even look like her now. We are supposed to be the last to recognise family resemblance in ourselves, but when I look in the mirror, I can see my mother looking back at me. Oscar Wilde was right and, when I realised this, it made me think of the influence that one generation has on the next.

Being a woman, I'm particularly conscious of this in the female line. There is no doubt that our values, our tastes, our manners are moulded by those who have gone before us in our family. We can break the mould or accept it. What matters to us is instilled in us by our upbringing. Some of us choose to continue the value system we inherited; some of us rail against it and embrace a totally different set of values.

My maternal grandmother was a major presence in our lives growing up because she lived to be 102 and also because her daughters were devoted to her, so my mother and my aunts spent a lot of time with her. Granny Dowdall was born in 1886. She was one of nine children and, by all accounts, was a competent, bright child. When other siblings came along and the living conditions were tight, she was sent to live with her grandparents in Newtown in Carlow, a few miles from the family home. I know that was common practice at the time, but it must have been difficult at some level to have been separated from parents and brothers and sisters. Not that it would have been spoken of but, nonetheless, it must have had some effect on the emotional and perhaps psychological well being of the person who was no longer in the family home. Granny grew up to be a very determined and strong-minded woman and perhaps the seeds for those qualities were sown in that child who went to live with her own grandmother at an early age.

She did well at school – primary school that is. There was no question of her being sent to secondary school. Her father was a local stonecutter and there was simply no money for that. But she did stay on after sixth class and became the teacher's helper. In effect, she became a primary-school teacher without going to college to train. She trained at the school of life. She had an expression that harks back to those days of walking barefoot to school and bringing fuel for the fire. Whenever any of us, her grandchildren, did well in a school test, she would always say, by way of congratulations, 'The sod of turf wasn't wasted on you.' It certainly wasn't wasted on her. Even in the latter years of her life, she could quote Shakespeare at will and her favourite poem was Goldsmith's 'The Village Schoolmaster', which she would recite from start to finish. It's a long poem, with lots of different themes, but Granny would go off into a world of contemplation and we would be enthralled 'that one small head could carry all she knew' (apologies to Oliver G!).

She had a great head for figures, too, and would have made a fine mathematician, and that gift she passed on to my mother and my auntie Eilish, who lived next door to us. Sadly it seems to have skipped a generation as I do not have a gift for maths and figures, but I do pride myself on knowing and loving a bargain. I would travel distances to pick up a bargain. The fact that the saving I've made on the item has probably been eaten up by the petrol it took to get to it is irrelevant. A bargain is a bargain after all!

Granny was married in 1911 at the age of twenty-five. She had seven children, two boys and five girls. When she was pregnant for the first time and her due date was approaching, she got up on a chair at the back wall of her house and called to the woman who lived next door. She had noticed big white aprons on the washing line in the garden and reckoned this woman was a midwife. She was right. 'So I engaged her,' she told us. And that was that. A practical, can-do sort of woman who got on with life. She never drank or smoked. She loved her home. Each of her daughters bought her a china tea set as a gift from their first week's wages when they left school and started working. She adored fine china and treasured those tea sets and her beloved Belleek ornaments. Her unmarried brothers who were working in Dublin would come to her for their dinners on Saturdays and Sundays. I can't imagine they got next, nigh or near the fine china!

Granny's life was not without its ups and downs. Her brother Peter was killed in 1922, during the Civil War. He was a private in the national army and was in a party of troops travelling from Wexford to Wellingtonbridge on 16 November. They had crossed Staplestown Bridge and Aughnagan Bridge with the aid of planks because both had been blown up by anti-Treaty insurgents. The patrol had just got back into the tender when they were ambushed by about fifteen men with two Thompson guns and some Peter the Painter automatic pistols. Granny's brother was the only man killed in the final volley. The inquest reported that he had a large wound, two inches long, situated about one inch below and behind the lower lobe of the right ear. There was no exit wound. His brother James, also a private in the army, identified the body and it was brought back to the family home in Fenagh, near Bagenalstown in County Carlow.

I remember Granny telling us about the coffin draped in the tricolour being laid across two chairs in the kitchen. How heartbreaking it must have been for his parents, both in their sixties, to see their son, the second youngest of their nine children, killed in this manner. His mother, my great-grandmother, died three years later in 1925, and his father the following year. The words of Commandant Gallagher, speaking at Peter's inquest on behalf of the military, proclaimed that the ambush was:

> '... *simply barbarous, happening in the county Wexford where men could not be found with pluck enough to fight the British when they were here. The gentlemen who were now fighting the national army were just coming out of the burrows into which the British terror drove them.*'

Tough words illustrating what was a most difficult and divisive time in Irish history. Granny was thirty-six when this tragedy struck her family. She was married with five children under the age of ten. It must have been a very sad and confusing time for her and her family to lose Peter in this way. He had fought against the British in 1916 and against the Black and Tans during the War of Independence. Granny told us stories of hiding guns for him and his comrades under the mattress in the baby's pram. What a tragedy for him then to be killed by one of his own countrymen in 1922.

Tragedy struck Granny's family again seven years later when her husband's sister took her own life. Anne Dowdall was forty-two years old at the time, a year younger than Granny. She was single, a farmer, living in the family home she had shared with her parents and her three sisters and four brothers at Windmill Hill in Rathcoole, County Dublin. Her parents were dead; her mother had passed in 1929 just two years before this tragedy occurred. A local man, who worked on the farm for Anne from time to time, found her lying in a pool of blood when he called to the house at six in the morning on Saturday, 24 August. There were two blood-stained knives beside her on the kitchen floor.

She told him she was cold and asked for a drink of water. The inquest reported that she died from shock and haemorrhage following a self-inflicted wound to the throat. A horrible tragedy for that poor woman and for her family. I have no doubt Granny was devastated by her loss. They were so close in age, and I know that Granny often brought her children to visit her husband's family farm in Rathcoole.

Granny was a great storyteller and spoke at length about those trips. She never once mentioned her sister-in-law's death, though. In those days, I suppose, it was something that wasn't spoken of. I wonder if my mother even knew about it.

The first I heard of it was when my cousin Barry who grew up next door to us in Clondalkin, began researching the family tree. It's often said that we don't know what goes on in families behind closed doors. That is so true. Sometimes we don't even know what's gone on behind our own family's door. That story is one of great sadness, of loss, of loneliness and of depression, all part of the human condition that goes to make us what we are.

Ten years after the tragic death of her sister-in-law, Granny lost one of her two sons to tuberculosis. Billy was twenty-six when he died at the Mater Hospital, having been a long-term patient at Peamount sanatorium. That was in 1939, and right through my childhood and her old age, she spoke with deep sadness about his loss. I cannot imagine the heartache she felt. Nor can I imagine the awfulness for my mother of losing her brother at such a young age. They were strong women certainly.

Granny lost her husband Chris in 1948. Both he and his son died on 8 December, the feast of the Immaculate Conception. The family had a deep faith and it would certainly have been a consolation to them that both father and son departed this life on such a significant date in the Catholic Church.

My grandfather was a labourer in Guinness' and I have to say the brewery looked after its employees' families really well. Until she died, Granny's medical requirements were taken care of and, on the day she turned 100, they sent a big bouquet of flowers, a cake, a bronze plaque of James's Gate – and a photographer to capture the moment for their in-house magazine. All this nearly forty years after their employee, Christopher Dowdall, had died. That was at a time when there was no talk of corporate social responsibility but it certainly suggests a sense of justice and caring on the part of that employer.

Granny's other son, my uncle Christy, named after his father, followed him into the Guinness Brewery. He married in 1950 and, on that day, he and his bride, Emily, left for Canada to begin a new life. The next time his mother saw him was seventeen years later when he, Emily and their three children came home for their first holiday in Ireland. I remember that visit so well. It was very exciting to have Canadian cousins around the house. They stayed a few days with all the relations. They had much nicer clothes and toiletries than we had – or so I thought anyway.

My abiding memory of that visit, though, is Granny. She would not let Christy out of her sight. She sat beside him at every gathering. She held his hand. She stroked his arm. She cried sitting beside him. She followed him from room to room. And she was inconsolable when, at the end of the fortnight's holiday, he and his family left to return to Canada.

To be honest, we Dublin-based grandchildren thought Granny was losing the plot. We could not understand all this carry on, and we sniggered at the good of it, wondering would she be tucking him up in bed next and reading him a bedtime story! Of course we had no understanding of what it must have been like to wave goodbye to a son on his wedding day and not see him again for seventeen years. All she had were letters and parcels at Christmas-time. No Skype or FaceTime. The odd, very odd, phone call. As a mother, I would find that heartbreaking. My heart ached when Lucy left for Korea at twenty-one. But I was out to visit her within months and she was home for Christmas and we spoke almost every day.

Granny had a lot of sadness in her life, living as a child away from the family home, losing her son and her husband in quick succession and losing her other son to emigration. Her first born, a daughter, had a troubled life also. She was extremely bright – she didn't lick that off the side of the road! She did really well in her exams and rose up through the ranks of the civil service. She would have prospered at university, too, but, once again, there was no money to move on to that level. Auntie Anna was also very talented. She won medals for singing and Irish dancing, even beating Maureen Potter into second place on one occasion. She sat exams for the English civil service and went to live in London for a while. But she was restless, unsettled and unhappy. She developed a fondness for alcohol. This was like a sword through her family's heart. Her mother, her father and all of her six siblings were pioneers. I know my mother worried a lot about her sister. I can't imagine what it was like for Granny to see her daughter struggling and falling more and more into addiction. Frightening, heartbreaking. She must have felt so helpless.

Granny was lucky to have such devotion from her other four daughters. I have no doubt Anna loved her mother dearly but she was not dependable. The others, Eilish, Phyllis, Kathleen and my mam, Pauline, were.

In Granny's later years, she was never alone. Kathleen lived with her and while she was out working, the others took it in turns to spend the day with Granny. She came to us in Clondalkin every Thursday. She'd have lunch in our house and tea in Auntie Eilish's next door. Or vice versa for a bit of variety! We loved Thursdays when Granny came. There'd be cakes, the fire would be lit in the sitting room and, of course, the good china would be used for the tea in her honour. Granny also came on holidays with us, so she was a major presence in our lives.

As I reflect now on the things that matter in my life, I realise the huge influence my grandmother and my mother have had on the woman that I am. For both of them, family was their rock, their responsibility, their joy and their sadness.

'Because I feel that, in the heavens above,
The angels, whispering to one another,
Can find, among their burning terms of love,
None so devotional as that of "Mother".'

Edgar Allan Poe

The apple doesn't fall far from the tree. My mother inherited so many of the qualities she witnessed in her mother. She also was devoted to her husband and her four children. Her best friends were her sisters. She was involved in her community. She was a stalwart of the Clondalkin ICA. She sang in the church choir and took

her turn on the church cleaning committee. She would chat for hours with her neighbours and she had many women friends from different stages of her life.

I always looked forward to the nights she would invite her former work colleagues from the College of Science for supper. Once again, the fire would be lit in the good room, the china would be out, there'd be tray cloths and doilies and sandwiches and cakes. My mother was a deeply loyal friend. I heard stories from people after she had died about problems they had confided to her. She went to the grave with those stories. She never divulged a confidence.

Mammy was strict also. She insisted on good manners, on working hard in school, on doing household chores, on coming in off the street when you were called. None of that went down well with us, her children, but that did not deter her one little bit. Daddy, on the other hand, was soft as putty and would always give in to our requests for extra time out playing on the days he was in charge. Good cop, bad cop scenario. It worked. None of us went off the rails. And hopefully there's a mixture of both their personalities in their adult children now. Sadness entered my mother's life when she was widowed at the age of fifty-eight. Daddy went to play golf on a work outing one Saturday morning and never returned. He died of a heart attack on the golf course. My mother is one of those people who has answered the door to the gardaí and received the saddest news ever. I don't think she ever fully recovered. Her consolation came from her family once again. She adored her grandchildren. She minded my children when I was working and would do anything to make life easier for me as a working mother. I would regularly come home to find the potatoes peeled and the table set for dinner and, pure bliss, the children's homework done.

I know I can attribute many parts of my personality and the way I live my life to the example of my mother and my grandmother. I'm practical, energetic, a can-do kind of person. In fact, the things that matter to me definitely came from them: family, faith, friendships, house and home. The value I place on these things didn't come all at once. It has evolved and I have come to treasure those parts of my life more and more.

My mother would be deeply touched that I like to recite the rosary as I go for power walks these days. Growing up, I hated having to say 'the prayers', as she called them, every evening after tea before you could watch TV or go out to play on a summer's evening. The rosary seemed interminable to me back then and was eating into valuable playtime. In actual fact, it probably took about ten minutes. Although, unlike other families, my mother insisted on the trimmings as well, Hail Holy Queen and the Memorare to name but some of the prayers.

Mammy never got to see that change of heart in me. It happened a few years after she died, while I was on pilgrimage in Medjugorje. The rosary was said a lot there and, every time, it would bring back memories of my mother. Not necessarily of her saying the rosary, but of her maybe sitting at the table drinking tea with Auntie Eilish, something they did every day after lunch. Or weeding in the back garden. Or whitewashing the front wall, which she liked to do, for some odd reason, almost every year. Saying the rosary in Medjugorje reminded me of the gentleness of my mother, of the simplicity of her life, its wholesome values and concerns. That feeling gave me comfort then and continues to give me comfort as I pound the pavement and recite the rosary.

There are other aspects of my mother's life that I'm beginning to recognise in my own as time passes and my children grow up and move on with their lives. I've already described her active, energetic, community- and family-based life, but there was another side to her life, too.

Sometimes when I called in to visit her, with my young children in tow, I would find her alone, sitting by the fire, quiet, lonely. I found it hard to reconcile this with the woman who for the most part was happily going about her business, running here, there and yonder. I remember on one occasion I suggested to her that she might enjoy reading a particular book that had just been published and her reply stopped me in my tracks, 'Mary, there are only so many books you can read.'

I could not relate to the loneliness that my mother felt. It was not part of my knowledge bank. I couldn't understand why she wouldn't get up and do something that would keep her busy and banish the blues. Now I understand what she was going through. My mother was on her own, without her life's partner, from the age of fifty-eight until she died aged eighty-three. I was separated and am divorced now for many years. I have found it increasingly difficult to settle into subsequent relationships and I now have times when I understand what my mother felt on those evenings when I called by. My life is full, interesting, stimulating. I love my work and I love my home and garden. There are, however, moments when I cannot summon up the enthusiasm, the motivation, to go out and water the plants, for instance, or to cook up a new recipe. A cloud descends. That cloud is loneliness. The kind of loneliness that overwhelmed me around Valentine's Day this year, as I will write about later. The kind of loneliness that comes from being without a partner in life. Like my mother, I have wonderful friends of both sexes. I value those friendships and I nurture them. I make the effort to keep in touch, to plan outings, to go places and do things. I relish the company of my friends, the conversations, the laughter and the tears.

That does not mean, however, that I'm immune to loneliness.

My children are grown up and organising their lives and I find myself increasingly alone because of my situation. There was a time when I would have been reluctant to admit to feeling sad and lonely – I would have felt that it was an admission of failure, of having a kind of non-life, of being bypassed in some way. I now recognise it as part of the human condition. As did the American novelist Thomas Wolfe:

> 'The whole conviction of my life now rests upon the belief that loneliness, far from being a rare and curious phenomenon, peculiar to myself and to a few other solitary men, is the central and inevitable fact of human existence.'

Loneliness is part of my story as it was part of my mother's story. It doesn't happen to me very often but I acknowledge that it will, quite possibly, feature more significantly in my life as the years progress. I imagine there are many who feel as I do but are reluctant to say so. I truly believe that when we name something as being a feature, a challenge, in our lives, it is somehow easier to deal with.

Certainly, loneliness is a part of the legacy that has passed from mother to daughter in my case, but so are strength, resilience, energy, love and happiness, all of which have seeped into my DNA through my grandmother and my mother. I wonder what legacy I am making to pass on to my children.

There is no doubt that they soak us up, our good qualities and our faults. I find it fascinating to meet adult children of friends after a number of years. These people that I knew as toddlers at picnics and kiddies' birthday parties have become uncannily like their parents. No pressure! But what a huge responsibility we take on when we bring children into the world. I know my children will absorb different aspects of my personality according to their own make-up. But absorb them they will. I'm conscious that my older daughter, Eva, is definitely a chip off the old block when it comes to house and home. Like me, she prefers the homewares section of shops to the clothes section. She's always buying candles and knick-knacks for the house. She has a real talent for arts and crafts – she didn't get that from me. She loves decorations – she definitely got that from me! In fact, I was away last Easter and told her to take the Easter decorations to her boyfriend's house. She sent me photos later on WhatsApp – she did a lovely job of decorating his house. I hope he thinks so too!

Lucy, the youngest, has inherited my wanderlust. I remember my mother's anxiety when I decided I wanted to teach English in France as soon as I left UCD, aged twenty-one. She just didn't want me to go. She was worried that I would be homesick and she would have preferred it if I had gone looking for a teaching job at home. I went anyway. She was right. I was desperately homesick at the beginning of my year away. I got over it, though, and had a wonderfully fulfilling, maturing experience. I would have stayed a second year but Daddy died suddenly on that golf outing, so I came home and got a teaching job in Coláiste Bríde, where I had gone to school myself. Lucy qualified in Social Science from UCD when she was twenty-one and took off to teach English in South Korea. She spent two years there and is now continuing the adventure in Australia.

Those are the obvious traits that my daughters have picked up from me. I'm very conscious, though, that they absorb subliminally as well. I would like them to be more confident than I was at their age. I want them to embrace life and take every opportunity that's offered to them, to be energetic and positive and kind and helpful to others. I want them to be happy in their personal lives and their relationships. Mind you, I want my two sons to have those qualities as well. And I think they do tick a lot of those boxes.

WHAT MATTERS

Oscar Wilde certainly got it right when he spoke about daughters emulating their mothers. But maybe we should rethink his view of the tragedy of sons.

I won't be around when my daughters reach my age. I wonder if they will look in the mirror one day and see me looking back at them. I wonder if they will feel, as I did at a certain stage in my life, that I had turned into my mother. I hope if they do that they're happy to be following in their mother's footsteps and taking on board the love and some of the value systems and traits that were around them as they were growing up. I know I'm happy to say that the best of me came from my mother and her mother before her.

'Thou art thy mother's glass, and she in thee
Calls back the lovely April of her prime.'
William Shakespeare

'All alone!
Whether you like it or not,
alone is something you'll be quite a lot!'

Dr Seuss

3.

Valentine Blues

Valentine's Day 2015

*'Don't grieve. Anything you lose comes
around in a different form.'*

Rumi

R ight now, I need convincing about the quotation above. I have come in from a walk with the dog. Forty minutes around the block and up to the green where he ran around like a whirling dervish, delighted to be out and feeling the wind through his recently groomed, though nonetheless substantial, coat. He was very happy and is now very tired and dozing on the couch. I, on the other hand, am anything but happy. I cried my way around that walk. I couldn't help it. The tears just came and trickled down my cheeks. I bowed my head when I was passing another walker and nobody was any the wiser. I just felt, and still feel, very sad and lonely.

I'm on my own today and finding it hard to cope with being alone. It's not always like this. My goodness, I lead a very full and busy life, for which I am thankful, but the cloud of sadness is hanging over me today. It's Sunday and I have no plans. There is nobody in the house but me, the dog and the two cats, and nobody will come through the door until tomorrow at least. I should have organised something to do today. I have to take control of this sadness, head it off at the pass and try to ensure that I don't put myself in this vulnerable position again.

Yesterday was Valentine's Day. And I'm happy to say that my children had a lovely day. I had spoken to Lucy and she told me she was going to a party. Eoin and his girlfriend got tickets to the Ireland-France Six Nations tie. Tom and his girlfriend headed off to spend the night in Glendalough to go walking today. Eva cooked dinner for her boyfriend in his house in Limerick. I am delighted for them all. I'm delighted that they are in happy relationships and that they have someone to romance and be romanced by on Valentine's Day. I settled in to spend the evening with a girlfriend here at my place. A nice informal meal and a catch up. She left at eleven and I went to bed content and with a huge sense of satisfaction. Not in a Mick Jagger kind of way! I was very satisfied and very grateful that my children were occupied romantically on Valentine's Day. It wasn't always thus. Last year, Lucy was away and two of them were single. This year, Lucy is still away but enjoying a stimulating adventure and the other three are all doing nice things on this special weekend. That made me happy because, as their mother, I'm happy if they're happy.

I feel at this point that I should clarify my position on Valentine's Day. I'm not a huge fan. I can take it or leave it. The flowers go up in price; the restaurants are too busy and not conducive to a good night out. The cards are expensive. Don't get me wrong. I have nothing against St Valentine, the man, although I do think it's a bit ironic that all this romance happens on the anniversary of the day in 269 when he was martyred in Rome: beaten with clubs and then beheaded. Valentine fell foul of the Emperor Claudius II by refusing to renounce his Christian faith and by continuing to marry Christian couples. And there we see the romantic connection. His association is not just with loved-up couples, though. As well as being the patron saint of love and young people and happy marriages, he is also beloved, if you'll pardon the pun, of beekeepers, travellers and the fainting. I suppose the latter could be as a result of romance – a bit of swooning is not uncommon, after all.

I'm touched by the fact that there are relics of St Valentine, including a vessel tinged with his blood, here in Ireland, in Whitefriar Street church in Dublin. They were given by Pope Gregory XVI in December 1835, as a token of esteem, to an Irish priest and famous preacher, Father John Spratt, following a sermon that he had given in Rome. Father Spratt was a Carmelite, a great champion of the poor in Dublin's inner city and the man responsible for the building of the Church of Our Lady of Mount Carmel, in Whitefriar Street.

The relics of St Valentine arrived in Ireland in November 1836 and, following a solemn procession through the streets of Dublin, were accepted into Whitefriar Street by the then Archbishop of Dublin, Archbishop Murray. When Father Spratt died, interest in the relics waned and they were put into storage only to re-emerge during renovation works in the 1950s. It was then that the shrine of St Valentine was built in Whitefriar Street church, a very popular spot with lovers – and the faithful, of course. In front of the shrine, there's a hardback copybook where people write their thoughts, their prayers, their worries, their thanks. Some of the entries are very moving. People entrusting their relationship to the care of St Valentine. Others praying for a loving partner. Mothers asking for his help for their children and their partners.

All very touching and comforting for the people involved and all a million miles from the way we mark Valentine's Day in the twenty-first century. Let's face it: it's all a bit contrived and forced and hugely commercial. Nice though for the 'young people'. As long as it's kept in proportion, of course, and people don't spend silly amounts of money that see them skint for the rest of the month.

It was a lot simpler when I was a teenager. Most things were! The lucky ones got an anonymous Valentine's card through the post in a red envelope, which was de rigueur so everybody in the house would know you'd got a card from a secret admirer.

I was never one of the lucky ones. I would go into school the next day and admire the cards that those who had been lucky would display proudly. And, of course, I'd feel sorry for myself.

I was very naïve back then. Why, oh why, did I not just send myself a card and pretend? With the insight and wisdom of age and maturity, I have my suspicions now about the origins of some of my classroom comrades' Valentine cards. Could they perhaps have bought and sent themselves a card? There's no doubt your standing in the group was greatly enhanced by the red envelope. Or perhaps a parent sent the odd card to a child back in the day? I know I was that soldier on occasions when my children were getting to the age where a Valentine card would give their confidence a bit of a boost and put a smile on their faces. It was lovely to see the sheepish grin as they opened the envelope and wondered who 'Guess Who?' was. All innocent fun. I must admit I did a double take one year when Lucy was about eight and came home from school chuffed to have received a Valentine gift from a boy in her class. When she took the red furry handcuffs out of her schoolbag, I didn't know whether to laugh or cry! You'll be pleased to learn that Lucy is twenty-three now and the handcuffs have remained unopened. They come down from the attic once a year with the other Valentine decorations and we display them on the mantelpiece. In their box!

People who know me know that I like to decorate my house. For all occasions. And Valentine's Day is no exception. There's the red tablecloth with hearts on it, the heart-shaped battery-powered lights, the red candles, the lipstick-patterned table napkins and lots more besides. I remember writing a chapter about Valentine's Day celebrations in my previous book, *Lines for Living*. That year, I cooked dinner for the family. Two of them had partners at the time. I was in my element: delighted to have the children around me, delighted to decorate the kitchen, delighted to serve spiced beef (you need to spice up your life around Valentine's Day) and a heart-shaped cake with bright-red icing. I remember that day so well. It was a Sunday. The French were in town for the Six Nations clash that had taken place the day before.

They were beaten by the Irish that year too. It was a lovely way to celebrate Valentine's Day. As was yesterday – a lovely way to celebrate, albeit very different. I drifted off to sleep in a warm glow of contentment that my children were happy.

So what happened to change all that between the time I went to bed and the time I woke this morning to a feeling of gloom and sadness? I felt empty. The thought of the day stretching out before me was almost unbearable. I wanted Sunday to be over so that I could wake up again and it would be Monday and I could get back to my busy life. And I cried. I felt so lonely. Had my life come to this? On my own.

I know that there will be more and more people-free days as life goes on. I cannot and do not depend on my children for my social life. I absolutely adore every occasion I spend with them, and I will be there for them always, but they have their own lives. They need and want to be with their own people. I accept that. So what do I do? I have to learn how to be in my own company. And to be happy that way. Most of the time, I am. I relish quiet time on my own in the house. Not today, though. It's oppressive and extremely sad. And pitiful. I hate the idea that people might feel sorry for me, and yet *I* feel sorry for me.

I'm reminded of my own mother being in this situation at times. I'd call in to her house and she'd be sitting there and I'd ask if anyone had called. I didn't need to ask, though. I knew the answer. She was sad and lonely. Her children were grown up and had their own lives and she was a widow. Little did she realise when she was rearing four children, cooking, washing, ironing, cleaning and having no time for herself, that there would come a day when she would be sitting alone, lonely.

Michael Harding, the Cavan writer who is also an accomplished actor and played The Bull McCabe in John B. Keane's classic *The Field*, wrote in a similar way about his own mother Nellie, who died in 2012 at the age of ninety-five. She was typical of a generation of Irish mothers who lived life in a very maternal and domestic way. Like my own mother, she had dedicated her life to her family and was happy to keep house for her husband and two sons, Michael and Brendan. In his book *Hanging with the Elephant*, Michael talks of his mother being very sad and lonely in her old age. An entry in her diary says it all really:

'Terrible lonely. No one called.'

I could see my own mother sitting on her own as I read those words. Both women had run busy, happy homes, cooking and cleaning and making things nice. As time moved on and the children moved away, they still wanted that life, that connection with people, that need to feel valued and useful, but it ebbed from them and left an emptiness and a loneliness in its place. Michael summed up this new reality very movingly:

'She reached out all her life to be held by others, because we all need to be held by something or someone. As she got older, that holding was less firm, and the friends dwindled until they were few and far between, and she realised that loneliness is what kills us all in the end.'

I spent a very pleasant day with Michael Harding in his mother's house in Cavan in the run up to Mother's Day. I had read *Hanging with the Elephant* and related to so much of what he said about the sadness of watching his mother alone and lonely in her old age, even down to the comfort he got from smelling her clothes after she had died. I couldn't part with my mother's favourite Aran cardigan and, to this day, it is still on the top shelf of my hot press. Her scent is long gone from it but it's a link to her still. Michael showed me around the now almost-empty family home that his mother and father had bought after their marriage and where they reared their family. We talked about the hall tiles that she had covered in carpet, the range where she cooked the meals, where every Sunday of his childhood she boiled a chicken in the manner in which her mother had taught her.

'If there was anything that signalled to me my mother's love and affection, it was the taste of chicken soup.'
Michael Harding

I saw photographs of the dining-room table, beautifully laid with a starched white tablecloth and china tea set to welcome visitors, and I saw photographs of happy gatherings in that room, plates piled high with dainty sandwiches and delicious-looking cakes. The table is still there but it's bare and the dining room is almost empty. We then moved into the sitting room where his mother had spent her old age, sitting in her favourite armchair, hoping that people would call. This tour of his old home became a piece for *Nationwide* that was broadcast on the eve of Mother's Day, a reminder of a generation of Irish mammies and a posthumous tribute to Mrs Harding. I hope she would have been pleased with it. She should have been very proud.

And now we've come full circle. I am part of the next generation of Irish mothers, but today I feel the same sadness as that older generation. For the first time, I understand properly my mother's sad days. It's a new stage in life that I am entering and that I must embrace. I realise I am not unique in this. I hope that by sharing this very real and painful emotion that others will feel a bit of consolation in the realisation that as we journey along life's path there will always be times of sadness. Nobody escapes. I suppose it's because we *are* loving human beings that we feel the sadness of being alone and longing for company at times. Another line from the poet Rumi springs to mind:

'Sorrow prepares you for joy. It violently sweeps everything out of your house, so that new joy can find space to enter.'

I look forward to that happening. In the meantime, I will galvanise myself against this sadness and devise strategies to deal with days like this. Writing down my thoughts here has definitely helped. I have passed a few hours of this long day. Tomorrow will be better. I will try to take on board the words with which I began this chapter – a strange quotation with which to begin a piece about Valentine's Day but it sums up how I feel: sad and lonely on the one hand but, on the other, realising that while I have lost, that which I have lost has its consolation for me as a mother. I will try not to grieve because what I have lost has indeed come round in another form. My children are happy and fulfilled and in love!

'Man cannot discover new
oceans unless he has the courage
to lose sight of the shore.'
André Gide

4.

Same Moon, Different Setting

'*Everybody has to leave, everybody has to leave their home and come back so they can love it again for all new reasons.*'

Donald Miller

I chose this quotation by Donald Miller for a very specific reason. Donald left his home in Texas at the age of twenty-one and travelled through the United States until he ran out of money – that happened in Portland, Oregon, and that is where he has lived since. He's now in his forties and a writer.

WHAT MATTERS

My youngest child, Lucy, left home at twenty-one also. I was thrilled for her setting off on an adventure but it broke my heart. I wrote about children leaving home in *Lines for Living* four years ago. At that stage, it was Eva, the eldest, leaving to share an apartment with a friend. About five miles down the road! That time, too, I was pleased for Eva, excited for her and Anna buying bits and pieces for their apartment, organising dinners and parties and breaking free. I was also lonely and sad and missed the chats.

I remember regretting that Eva, Lucy and I would no longer have our Tuesday date nights, in the jammies with tuna in pitta bread and tea, watching *Grey's Anatomy*.

I wrote about the empty nest, the end of family life as we had come to know it, new beginnings, new adventures, the way we rear our children so that they can take flight with confidence.

Little did I know then that what lay ahead in terms of leave-taking and new beginnings would strike me at the core of my being and confirm to me that, despite the full, varied and stimulating life that I enjoy, what matters to me most is the well being of my children. This has been the case since the day they were born and I have now resigned myself to the fact that my mother was right. We never, ever stop worrying about our offspring. They may leave the nest, they may travel to far-flung places, they may embark on wonderful adventures but they never leave your heart.

In 2012, Lucy graduated from UCD with an honours degree in Social Science. She had decided she didn't want to continue studying and perhaps do a Master's so in her final few months of college, as well as preparing for her exams, she completed a diploma online to teach English as a foreign language. I was the one who alerted her to that course of action. As you know, I love a bargain and I subscribe to the odd voucher site on my phone. One fine day in early 2012, I noticed this online TEFL course at a knock-down price. It was a real bargain and Lucy, Tom and Eva all bought the voucher and completed the course. *Always nice to have in the back pocket*, I thought. That's where it has remained in Eva's and Tom's cases. Lucy took the qualification very carefully out of the back pocket and set it centre stage after she finished her degree. She had decided she wanted to travel, so she researched teaching opportunities abroad. She had her degree and she had her TEFL diploma so she was qualified to teach English as a foreign language. South America was an option for her. She had studied Spanish at school and liked the idea of travelling there. She settled on South Korea, though, did several interviews and was accepted as a teacher. I was surprised at her choice of country until Lucy told me that the education authorities in South Korea would pay her airfare and also provide her with an apartment rent free. Like mother, like daughter, I suppose. She couldn't pass up a bargain like that! The great saving was offset in my head, though, by the fact that thousands were spent on her college education and yet her first job came from a ninety-nine euro voucher!

A busy few months followed with visa applications, amassing endless documents, Christmas, going-away parties and last-minute shopping, and then the day dawned in February 2013 when it was time to drive Lucy to the airport. Despite the rushing around of the previous few days and the making of endless cups of tea for people calling to say goodbye to wish Lucy well with little cards and gifts, a feeling of nausea had been developing in my stomach. I actually thought I was coming down with something after all the racing and chasing but the night before she left, as I lay in bed, unable to sleep, contemplating Lucy not being in the bedroom next door to mine from the following morning, I understood what that feeling was. It was heartache, the kind you feel in the pit of your stomach, that churns around like the drum of a washing machine.

I kept my counsel, though. I didn't want to rain on Lucy's parade as she set off, on her own, on this adventure that would take her to a very different part of the world and introduce her to a new culture, a whole new life experience.

She was to travel alone to Dubai and then on to Seoul, where she would be met and transported by bus for several hours to her destination. I'm sure she was nervous at the prospect of this journey, with all her luggage and no travelling companion. We focused on the positives, though, the adventure, the excitement, the possibilities and opportunities. And that worked fine until it came to the moment for her to go through security. I can still see her walking away from me in her patterned leggings and her khaki jacket, pulling her carry-on bag behind her. I thought my heart would quite simply burst out of my chest with love and the desire to just hold her one more time. I was bereft. I couldn't get my head around the fact that I didn't know when I would see her again.

It was raw grief that I felt. My daughter, my twenty-one-year-old, my baby, was emigrating. I was conscious that she had chosen to leave Ireland. I cannot imagine the grief of a mother whose child would rather stay and work at home but has to leave. That's an added sadness. Thomas Malthus, the eighteenth-century British cleric and expert in population and demography, described that sadness accurately:

'A great emigration necessarily implies unhappiness of some sort or other in the country that is deserted.'

I remembered my grandmother and the fact that her son Christy emigrated on his wedding day to start a new life in Canada. What a bitter-sweet occasion that wedding must have been. Did she realise it would be seventeen years before she hugged him again? I was feeling limp and panicky because I would have to wait a day or two to get a text from Lucy to say she had arrived safely. And then there would be Skype and FaceTime and WhatsApp.

None of this mattered at that moment of leave-taking, though. All I felt was the space that was opening up between me and my daughter as she disappeared past the security desk.

I cried on the way home until I was exhausted and headachy and could cry no more. The floodgates opened again when I went into Lucy's bedroom and opened the wardrobe to see all the empty hangers that had been bursting with her clothes for so many years. The quietness, the emptiness, the sadness seemed all consuming. There was me a few years ago, regretting the Tuesday-night tuna and telly with Eva and Lucy, and Eva was just a few miles away. This was serious stuff. Lucy had gone to Korea.

She and Eva are very close as sisters and spent a lot of time together before Lucy left. They had said their goodbyes the night before because Eva was working and couldn't go to the airport, and when Lucy came down to the kitchen there was a note from Eva congratulating her on taking this brave step and saying she was proud to have her as a sister. This was certainly a brave step for Lucy, a new beginning, but it also, of necessity, marked the end of an era of sisterly closeness for Eva and Lucy in their twenties.

'A sister is a gift to the heart, a friend to the spirit, a golden thread to the meaning of life.'
Isadora James

Things would never be the same again. The same is true of Lucy's love for and closeness to her brothers. Tom and Eoin missed her deeply when she left and she missed them.

Once again I realised that relationships are what matter in every aspect of our lives. Frederick Buechner, the American Presbyterian Minister, writer and theologian described the sweet sorrow of parting well:

'You can kiss your family and friends good-bye and put miles between you, but at the same time you carry them with you in your heart, your mind, your

*stomach, because you do not just live in a world but
a world lives in you.'*

The wound of separation healed, the sadness passed,
slowly. Lucy got settled, slowly. And a most wonderful
life-enhancing experience opened up and blossomed
for her. After a ten-day orientation course in Seoul, she
was assigned a teaching post in Sejong, a brand-new city
built up around decentralised government departments.
The school was new also, welcoming its first intake of
100 secondary-school students. It had state of the art
facilities and, because it was located in this new city
where there was very little infrastructure, Lucy was
offered a room on the campus. That did not go down
well and she reminded her employers of the deal: her
own apartment. In fairness to the school authorities, they
were trying to be helpful. All of the permanent Korean
staff, some of them married with families in other parts
of the country, were living on campus because of the
remoteness of the location. And it was remote. When
Lucy was finally housed in her apartment in Jochiwon,
a small rural town, her daily commute involved a forty-
minute bus ride followed by a thirty-minute walk to work
and the reverse on the way home. For her, it was worth

it. I admired her ability to speak up for herself so soon after she had arrived and felt it augured well for her first foray into independence.

Pride and relief took hold of my heart at that point and Lucy settled into her new life extremely well. She took Korean lessons, which involved learning a whole new alphabet - Hangol. She made great friends from different parts of the world and she immersed herself in the local culture.

She didn't forget her own culture though, and joined the Daegu Fianna GAA club. There is no doubt that the worldwide GAA family provides a wonderful link with home for the increasing numbers of Irish people living in different parts of the world. 'The savage loves his native shore' and it's a great comfort for the emigrant to have that connection with his native shore through the GAA. It's also a great comfort for the emigrant's family in Ireland to know that welcome is there for their son or daughter when they arrive in new places, far away from home. It was lovely to see Lucy's GAA jersey with her name written in Hangol on the back. And the Daegu Fianna enjoyed some success in their Asian league while she was a member, which added to the thrill for her family back home.

Six months after Lucy landed in Korea, I went out to visit her. I was hyper during the ten-hour flight from Dubai to Seoul, dying to hold her, wondering what it would be like to walk through the arrivals door and see her standing there. It was, as you would expect, wonderful, very emotional, so good to hug her after months apart. I got a real insight in that moment into why my granny wouldn't let her son out of her sight when he came back to Ireland for a holiday after seventeen years in Canada. I just wanted to spend every waking and sleeping moment with my daughter.

She was a great tour guide and had organised trips to beautiful and interesting places all over South Korea. There were palaces in Seoul, tea rooms and folk villages, seaside and sand sculptures in Busan, a visit to the UN memorial to Korean troops who lost their lives in the Korean War in the fifties, nights out with her friends at Korean barbecues, which would not be a feature of any visit to Lucy today because her diet is now totally vegan. She introduced me to chai latte, for which I have developed an enduring fondness and I can tell a good one from a mediocre one. (I would describe it as a tea equivalent of a cappuccino with cinnamon and sugar added. Go for the skinny option and you offset the sugar with the low-fat milk!)

I was very impressed with the way my youngest child had matured into a capable, independent young woman in such a short space of time. I allowed myself a little pat on my parental back. This was a moment of affirmation for me that the way she had been brought up worked and that knowledge is a great gift. We do our best rearing our children and the fact that they turn into good, capable adults matters hugely to us.

While we are rearing them, though, we can have huge self-doubt about how we are doing. We are doing our best. We need to remember that and not be so hard on ourselves.

The highlight of my trip to Korea was a visit to Lucy's school in Sejong. Yes, I did the early morning bus ride and walk and the walk and bus ride at the end of the day, and I take my hat off to her for doing it five days a week in winter and summer, rain, hail, snow and, worst of all, dreadful humidity.

Sejong Global High is state of the art. The Korean government puts great store by schooling and considers a good education system crucial to socio-economic success. It's not for nothing that they have become one of the fastest growing economies in the world and have been praised by world leaders, including Barack Obama, for their education system. If Sejong Global High School is anything to go by, that praise is richly deserved. Eighty-five per cent of students leaving high school go on to third level. And my goodness but they have lots of universities to choose from. In Daejon, a city the same size as Dublin, there are no fewer than sixteen universities. Is it any wonder that sixty-five per cent of Koreans in their mid-twenties hold at least a primary degree?

There was a very proud Irish mammy walking the corridors of Sejong Global High that day. I was introduced to the school principal and to Lucy's colleagues in the English department. They all sang her praises loudly, as did her students when I visited them in their classrooms. I even taught a class, which I would like to say brought me back to my own teaching days but that would be very far from the truth.

The facilities that these teachers and students have at their disposal are tremendous. Every primary and secondary school in this country of 50 million people has high-speed fibre optic broadband. Every student has digital textbooks. I visited the music department and walked around the instruments: twenty-one guitars, violins, keyboards and other instruments that I can't remember. When I say twenty-one I don't mean the total number. Not at all. There were twenty-one of each instrument. Why? Because there are twenty-one students in each class. Wouldn't Irish music teachers think they'd died and gone to heaven if they walked through those rooms? And what a wonderful opportunity for those students who don't pay school fees but who are chosen for a school such as Sejong Global High, depending on their academic ability. As you can imagine, the competition is fierce and the students who are selected work really hard during their time in boarding school.

'Really hard', as we understand the term in Ireland, doesn't come close to describing the workload of these

Korean students. Lessons begin at 8.30. There is a short mid-morning break, a lunch break, an afternoon break and a dinner break. Lessons and study take up the whole day, with students getting to bed sometimes at eleven thirty. Every high-tech classroom has three tall circular tables at the back of the room, the kind we'd see in hotels for the drinks reception before a function, nicely dressed with a long white tablecloth and a bow under the table top to pinch in the fabric and give it a nice shape. There are no cloths or bows on these tables in Korean secondary-school classrooms. They do have a specific function, though. When students feel overcome with tiredness and their eyelids are getting heavy, they leave their desks and stand for a while at the high tables to prevent themselves from falling asleep. This happens a lot when there are house exams looming and the students stay up later and later to study.

When I taught one of Lucy's classes that day, two young boys took to the tables at the back of the room. I know what you're thinking. I was sending them to sleep with my rabbiting on. I did check with Lucy afterwards and there were exams scheduled for the following week. Phew!

Schooling is taken very seriously in Korea, by the teachers, the parents and the students. They want to get good results. They are motivated and accept the hard work during term and relax totally with their families and friends during the holidays. I suppose it's a question of what matters most at different stages in our lives. Those students were happy to have Lucy teaching them and were very sorry to see her move on to a different city and a different school at the end of a year. She chose to move to Daegu and get experience in a primary school, which was a fifteen-minute subway ride from her apartment. That must have been bliss! At the end of the second year, Lucy left Korea and moved to Australia. The adventure continues.

My twenty-one-year-old daughter is now twenty-four. She has travelled to Korea, Japan, Vietnam, Australia and those travels have afforded her wonderful opportunities. Mary Anne Radmacher, the American author and artist who wrote the inspirational book *Lean Forward into Your Life*, could have been describing Lucy when she said:

> *'I am not the same, having seen the moon shine on the other side of the world.'*

What a lovely thought. I am delighted for Lucy because she has met people from different parts of the world, gained insights into different cultures and learned how to organise the day-to-day running of her life with shopping, utility bills, leases, transport systems, the lot. Most of all, though, she has matured into a competent, thoughtful, concerned and compassionate human being with a lively interest in environmental and humanitarian affairs. And that's what matters. She is living her life to the full and although I miss her every day, and there's an empty place at the table and in our hearts, I'm delighted for her.

I'm also delighted for Eva, Tom and Eoin, who maintain a busy and loving relationship with their sister through social media. To see the look of joy on their faces when they are reunited at Christmas time is a privilege, particularly last Christmas when Lucy, due home on St Stephen's Day, walked up the driveway on Christmas Eve to surprise us. Boy did she succeed there. A moment we will treasure as a family always. A reminder that no matter how routine and busy our daily lives are, and how far apart we may be from each other in practical terms, the special moments, like Lucy's homecoming on Christmas

Eve, are indelibly linked to personal relationships with loved ones – and I look forward to the next one.

And I also look forward to the day in the future when Lucy, having left her home, comes back to it and loves it again for all new reasons. I'm excited at the very thought of that.

'I was brought up a Catholic,
so I take no pleasure in guilt.'

Imelda Staunton

5.

The Guilty Glass

'*The wound is the place where the Light enters you.*'

Rumi

I hope Rumi is right because I feel wounded today. I am not happy with myself and I look forward to Light replacing this wounded feeling before too long.

I woke up this morning feeling sluggish, a bit groggy. I didn't have a good night's sleep. That's not unusual, in fairness. I have never been a good sleeper. The slightest worry or anxiety will see me tossing and turning for hours, and the worry will be magnified a hundredfold during those dark, lonely hours when the demons take over from rational thought. I will imagine the worst-case scenario and wish for sleep to come or the night to give way to the morning. The person who said the darkest hour is just before the dawn wasn't lying. I know it's said to give hope and a realisation that things will improve, but the darkness of that last hour is deeply upsetting and horrible. The following morning, I always chide myself as to how silly I was to allow those thoughts to take over my brain, and as I embark on the routine of daily life, all order is restored and the worry has shrunk to a manageable problem that I can and do deal with.

This morning is different. I drank a fair bit of wine last night. I found it very hard to write those words. I am embarrassed. I dislike myself for being in this position. I should qualify this revelation by saying that I'm on a few days away with friends and the daily routine consists of a forty-five-minute power walk at eight in the morning to get the day off to a good start. Then there is breakfast with six people gathered around the table chatting about anything and everything. The atmosphere is very relaxed and convivial and there are a lot of laughs. The day unfolds then with a trip to a place of interest, the reading of books, a bit of grocery shopping, cups of tea or coffee, normal holiday fare, until six o'clock when the sun has gone over the yard arm and it's '*le moment de l'aperitif*', as the French so delicately refer to the time when we sit down and have a glass of wine and some nibbles. Nothing wrong with that, of course.

It's actually a very civilised way to welcome the evening. You have a shower, put on the glad rags and a bit of make-up then regroup with the pals and sit around chatting and enjoying a glass of wine before heading out for dinner. Except it's never a glass, it's two glasses, and then there's wine with dinner and then perhaps a nightcap, which, in my case, is aptly named because one thing it certainly does is put the cap on the night and any chance of proper sleep. I toss and turn and the demon of guilt seeps into my head and when I rise in the morning, it's still there as my companion for the day. Unlike the worries or anxieties about work or family that diminish and become manageable with the dawn, the guilt that follows wine remains solid for the day.

I know there are many people who will read this and say, 'What is she on about?' They will take account of the fact that the day begins with a serious bout of exercise followed by activity and conversation and healthy eating and that there's no wine produced before six o' clock. They will acknowledge that this is holiday time and, if they realise that I don't drink during the week when I'm at home, they'll think I'm gone in the head altogether. They will advise me to get over myself, to lighten up, to relax and enjoy myself.

We all have our reservations about different beverages. Ronald Reagan jokingly said he never drank coffee at lunchtime because he was afraid it would keep him awake for the afternoon. And wasn't it Benjamin Franklin, one of the founding fathers of the United States, a brilliant scientist, mathematician and inventor, who suggested:

'In wine there is wisdom, in beer there is freedom, in water there is bacteria.'

I am not a Moany Mary. I do enjoy myself. But I also suffer pangs of guilt and a slight depression following a night like last night. My companions don't suffer the same slings and arrows. They, too, enjoy themselves.

Some of them feel a bit sluggish today, but they don't feel guilty. They don't feel they've let themselves down in some way.

I have to admit I seem to be hard-wired for guilt. I am by and large a very positive person. I look on the bright side of things for the most part. But I succumb to guilt quite easily. Is it Catholic guilt? I don't think so. All of my companions on this break are Catholic and they certainly feel no guilt! For me, guilt and regret are closely aligned. I could say I regret the fact that I drank a lot of wine last night but that is quite simply skirting around the issue and does not adequately describe the way I feel today. It's not a strong enough emotion in this instance. Sometimes it fits the bill. I feel guilt, as in regret, that I didn't spend more time with my mother in her final years. I was very busy with a job and four school-going children, but if I had the time back again I would not allow her to be sitting lonely in her own house in the evenings.

To be honest, I think my penchant for guilt comes from my mother in some ways, particularly with regard to drink. She hated alcohol with a vengeance and it's not just that the taste didn't appeal to her. I remember her telling me that she was very anaemic as a young woman and the doctor recommended that she take a spoonful of stout every day. She did what she was told the first day but did not like the taste and that was the end of that. (She must have found some other way of increasing her iron intake because she was a very healthy woman for the rest of her life until she became ill with cancer at the age of eighty-one.)

However, her abhorrence of the taste of alcohol was only in the ha'penny place compared to her hatred of the notion of drink and the damage it could do to people. Mam was a member of the Total Abstinence Association, a pioneer all her life. If she had taken the stout, it would have been purely for medicinal purposes. Her mother and three of her sisters were pioneers too. Her fourth sister had a problem with alcohol. I can understand that this would have coloured her view of people drinking. She was never comfortable in a situation where there was drink. You could always sense her disapproval. My father was not a pioneer, although if he had a whiskey on Christmas Day and a beer once or twice during his holidays that would be the height of it. He was a hard-working man and there was little money to spare for drink when we were growing up. I'd say even if he had been gasping for a drink, though, it would not have been worth the disapproving looks that Mam would have thrown in his direction.

There was nearly a diplomatic incident at the time of my twenty-first birthday. I'm the eldest in the family and my parents were throwing a party for me in the house. This was uncharted territory for my parents and for my aunt and uncle next door, who would be doing the same thing for my cousin William three months later. Dad went to a lot of trouble, getting in extra chairs, cleaning windows, having the piano tuned. Mam and Auntie Eilish prepared the food, simple fare but very nicely done. We had cocktail sausages, of course, rasher and egg pie (very fashionable in the seventies!), every kind of sandwich imaginable and lots and lots of gorgeous cakes. And then there was the question of drink: to serve or not to serve alcohol.

My mother was adamant that there would be no alcoholic beverages served to young people in her house. I was turning twenty-one, remember. My father pleaded the case on behalf of the people who would be there who

were well past that age, like married cousins or older brothers and sisters of some of my friends who had been invited. There was a lot of toing and froing. It would have put Kofi Annan or George Mitchell to the pin of their collar to resolve the impasse at one point.

White smoke emerged from the chimney at the eleventh hour, the day before the party, when Mam agreed that the older people at the party could have a drink but not anyone up to twenty-one. And that included me. And so it was.

It was a great party. We ate, didn't drink and sang till the wee small hours. I do think, though, that my introduction to adulthood and the manner in which the question of alcohol was handled may have had some impact on the guilt I have felt around it ever since. Three months later, William's twenty-first was held next door and there was beer at it for anyone who wanted it. The floodgates had been allowed to open.

Despite the dry twenty-first birthday party, alcohol has been a part of many celebrations since I became an adult. I lived in Brittany for a year and enjoyed an occasional glass of wine when my flatmate Jill and I could afford it, which wasn't very often. We were both teaching English at the Université de Haute Bretagne in Rennes and our tipple of choice was a mug of cider when we treated ourselves to the wonderful Breton crêpes on a night out. Innocent times certainly.

When I returned from Brittany, I lived at home until I got married so there was no fear of a drink there with my mother standing guard over an empty drinks cabinet. There was wine at my wedding, a glass and a top-up for all guests and a glass for the toast. That was the norm in 1982 and, once again, it was all we could afford. I never drank when I was pregnant or breastfeeding so that took care of four years. Other than that, there would have been a shared bottle of wine on a Saturday night or a bit more at a dinner party.

There is no doubt, though, that as the years go by and the children are reared, the wine flows more freely. There is also no doubt that alcohol consumption among Irish women is reaching a worrying level. It's been happening since the mid-nineties when teenage girls were matching teenage boys glass for glass. That might be a nice thumbs-up for the notion of equality between the sexes but the fact of the matter is that, metabolically and hormonally, females are different and can develop alcohol-related problems more easily than males. The fact that wine has got so cheap doesn't help. Neither does the fact that we all associate bubbles, as we euphemistically refer to Champagne and Prosecco, with celebration. It's far from bubbles we were reared, but they also have become more affordable and we can't get enough of them.

'Three be the things I shall never attain: envy, content, and sufficient Champagne.'
Dorothy Parker

I am no different to anybody else. I love the feeling of relaxation in sharing a glass of wine with a friend at the end of the day. I love raising a glass of bubbles and clinking to celebrate a birthday or an anniversary or anything at all. It bothers me, though. I drink away with the pals and then when I go to bed I fall asleep only to wake up a few hours later and spend the rest of the night trying to keep the demon guilt at bay, knowing that I will be feeling annoyed with myself and depressed the following day.

I sound as if I'm never without a glass in my hand or that I go around with my head tilted backwards in case I'd spill some of the drink I have consumed. Neither is true. When I'm at home and working, I don't drink. It just doesn't arise. I enjoy gatherings with friends where there is no alcohol served. In fact, one of the best parties I was at in recent years was a surprise sixtieth for a friend. It was a lunch followed by a *céilí* and the only drinks served were water, orange juice and tea. It was a wonderful celebration, great fun and nobody missed the drink, least of all me.

I enjoy going to lunches with friends where I drive myself and I know therefore that I will not have even one glass of wine. That's a rule that I never break. The fact that I am not having a glass of wine doesn't take from the enjoyment one little bit. My difficulty is that, sometimes, when I am in a situation where there is drink served, I, like many other people, drink more than I would like.

Unlike many other people, I suffer the post-event guilt and self-loathing and this is the first time I have said this openly, even to myself.

I have great admiration for people who decide that they have had enough of drinking and give it up altogether. I have a friend who came back from three weeks' holiday in France with her husband and decided she needed a break from wine. She said she was tired of having a glass at lunchtime and feeling sleepy after it and then having more in the evening. She wanted to give her system a break. That was seven years ago and she hasn't touched a drop of wine since, she doesn't miss it one little bit either. I asked her would she not like a glass of Champagne at a wedding or on Christmas Day, bubbles being such a feature of those celebratory gatherings. She said, rightly, that this is a myth and that it just doesn't enter her head anymore.

I have a male friend who doesn't drink at all either. And he's French. Not too many of them about, French people who don't touch a drop of wine! He is excellent company at a dinner or a party, always looking out for others and the first to rise from the table to lend a hand in the kitchen. He loves food and has recommended some excellent restaurants in different parts of the world but never has a glass of wine. He enjoys the chat and is the last to leave to go home and one of his most endearing features is his patience with people as the night goes on and they all become hilarious in their own eyes.

I wonder if I would be content to never drink again. I don't think so. I know there is a woman who would be looking down from heaven with a smile on her face if I could. I would miss the conviviality of sitting down and relaxing and chatting with friends over a glass of chilled wine. My problem is around the guilt which seems certain to have had its genesis in my mother's attitude to alcohol. I am going to embark on a period of total abstinence and see how it feels – and more importantly see how *I* feel. I will revisit this chapter then and report on the results of my experiment. I will allow the light to gain entry through the wound. There is another line from Rumi that poses a question for me. I will use it as my mantra over the next few days:

'Why do you stay in prison, when the door is so wide open.'

WHAT MATTERS

A month has passed since that day of wounded self-loathing and guilt. I drank water and Diet Coke for the remainder of the break away with my pals. I have to say it was not difficult. Once I've made up my mind about something I am pretty determined. I give up sweet things for Lent without too much difficulty. A bit of mortification is good for the soul, they say. My soul must be gleaming by now. I haven't had a glass of wine in several weeks and I haven't missed it at all. Great, you'll say. *You're not waking up in the middle of the night with guilt-ridden and anxious thoughts.* Not true. The anxiety is still there. I have come to accept that it's part of my disposition. I will always find something to gnaw over in that darkest hour before the dawn.

I have come to accept that as we get older, we are more predisposed to unhappy thoughts. Maybe it's because we're not racing around trying to get children out to school on time or trying to build a career or navigate a relationship. We have more time on our hands, time to ruminate, to worry about silly things, to feel lonely. Our lives are changing. If we have children, they have become adults. Our careers are settled, reaching their conclusion in many cases. It's time to take stock. I have always said that if I had the years when my children were small back again I would relish them. I wouldn't be taking the opportunity when they were occupied with play or food to get some chores done. I would sit with them, enjoy their company and worry about filling the washing machine later.

I have lovely memories of when my children were small but as the sometimes controversial American children's author Lois Lowry points out:

'The worst part of memories is not the pain. It's the loneliness of it. Memories need to be shared.'

Ageing brings with it the need for adjustment and for acceptance of the good things and the sad things that go with that territory. I accept that there will be more loneliness in my life. I saw it enter my mother's life as she got older and I didn't understand her melancholy. Now I do. I accept that I will have days when I find it hard to motivate myself to embrace the new day. I try to be positive but sometimes it takes a lot of effort. I have great admiration for Oprah. She is a woman with a wonderfully positive attitude to life. I wish I felt like she does when she wakes up:

'Every morning when I open my curtains for that first look at the day, no matter what the day looks like – raining, foggy, overcast, sunny – my heart swells with gratitude. I get another chance.'

My heart doesn't always swell with gratitude. Sometimes, it flutters anxiously. I do appreciate, though, that I get another chance. And I take that chance. There is no doubt that the physical act of getting out of bed improves the mood instantly. There's something about being vertical which makes challenges seem more manageable. What matters is that we should accept the melancholy and the loneliness and not feel a failure for having those thoughts.

As a generation, I feel we are very hard on ourselves. Both of my parents left school after their Inter Cert and worked really hard to give their four children the very best they could afford. They dedicated their lives to their family and their community. They did their best always. So many couples of their generation did exactly the same. They were of their time. The realisation of the sacrifices they made brings a responsibility to us, their children, to make the most of our lives. We had

so many opportunities that were beyond our parents'
wildest dreams. We too have done our best. We should
acknowledge that and also acknowledge our weaknesses
and the changes that life brings.

I look at people who are maybe ten years younger than me
who are still at the rushing-around stage of life, ferrying
children, hurrying to and from work, shopping at the
weekends, wishing for some time to relax. They don't
realise that the next stage is certainly more relaxing and
less rushed, but it brings with it some low moments that
are never anticipated. I am a very lucky woman. I lead a
full, varied and stimulating life. I love my work and I have
come to accept that life includes moments of great joy
and also moments of sadness and loneliness. You can't
really understand one without the other. Knowing that
there are two sides to the coin is an advantage, as is the
realisation that we all go through this stage in life. I have
yet to meet somebody who is happy all the time. I have
met many people who say they are, but I don't believe
them. They tend to be people who care about what others
think and who want others to believe that their lives are
perfect. That's sad in itself. It's ironic to think that they
might actually be happier if they admitted to moments
of sadness and loneliness.

On a positive note, Martha Beck, the renowned sociologist and life coach who I have come across through the column she writes in Oprah's magazine, says that:

'Loneliness is proof that our innate search for connection is intact.'

I couldn't agree more. Connection and involvement with other people are, for me, some of the joys of life.

Another joy of this stage of life is that I am not influenced by what others think of me. I have my beliefs and my values – and, sure, isn't it the fact that we're all different that makes life interesting? I'm glad that my day of self-loathing has opened up into this examination of some of the emotions and states of being that I have encountered as I have lived and loved, won and lost.

I have been very honest with my thoughts about the proverbial glass of wine. Knowledge is power and I know that a couple of glasses of wine to celebrate with friends is fine but several will bring on the guilt that seems to be in my genes. For the most part, I am very mindful of this. I shall be mindful of it all the time from now on. The consequences of not being mindful are, for me, to be avoided. I take consolation from the fact that Louis Pasteur, the man who brought pasteurisation and with it improved health into the world in the eighteenth century, referred to wine as the 'most healthful and most hygienic of beverages'. Like mother's milk! I don't think so!

I began this chapter with the words of Rumi and I quoted him as I ended my first guilt-ridden writing session. Those words about wounds and prisons definitely suited my mood then. I think it fitting to end with the words of this eminent twelfth-century Persian poet. This is a piece I came across in the intervening month. If I had seen it as I woke up on that fateful day a month ago, I might have felt better about myself:

> *'Either give me more wine, or leave me alone.'*
> *Rumi*

*'When I eat with my friends,
it is a moment of real pleasure,
when I really enjoy my life.'*

Monica Bellucci

6.

A New York Easter

'Awake thou wintry earth,
Fling off thy sadness!
Fair vernal flower, laugh forth
Your ancient gladness.'

Thomas Blackburn

The lines above, from the British poet Thomas Blackburn's 'Easter Hymn', epitomise for me the joy of Easter, a time of hope, of celebration, of affirmation. As I get older, I look forward to Easter more. I find it meaningful and special.

Growing up, Easter came at the end of a long and tedious Lent topped off by an even longer, metaphorically speaking, Holy Week. I always gave up sweets for Lent. My mother gave me a tin box in which to collect them, so that I would have a stash to gorge on when Easter Sunday finally arrived. By the end of Lent that box contained an assortment of wrapped and unwrapped boiled, chocolate and other sweets, some stuck to each other, particularly the ones that I had taken out and sucked when the temptation got too much and Satan refused to 'get behind me'.

Holy Week presented an interminable litany of compulsory spring cleaning and trips to the church. The reward was the wearing of a new dress and snow-white ankle socks for the first time that year to Easter Sunday mass. The socks heralded the start of summer in our young heads. We must have been hardy bucks or else the weather was milder back then because any Irish parent who would send their child out in ankle socks at Easter these days and leave them in them from then until September should be hauled up for neglect or cruelty.

After Easter mass, the day was spent eating lots of chocolate and the haul of saved sweets. That was it really. There was no fancy dinner, no Easter decorations, no going away for the long weekend.

The first Easter decorations I got came from the mother of a German au pair who minded my children in the nineties. They celebrate Easter very nicely in Germany. Lots of wreaths and egg-shaped baubles and fluffy chicks and bunnies around the house. An egg-painting session at the kitchen table on Easter Saturday. Great fun and it certainly beats the pants off washing windows and polishing silver! Children also help make a sponge cake in an Easter Bunny mould which is placed in a basket at the foot of the altar on Easter morning at mass and blessed by the priest before being brought home and given pride of place on the Easter table. The priest's final duty at the end of mass is the announcement of a chocolate-egg hunt in the church grounds, which sees all the children making a dignified but hasty retreat out the church door to start foraging for chocolate gold! My children loved those German traditions and there's always been a nice, simple and colourful celebration of Easter in our house.

As you can imagine, given my well-documented penchant for decorations of any shape or hue, I have added to my Easter collection over the years. And I have many happy memories of Easter lunches with family – the white tablecloth decorated with daffodils, a present from Germany, real daffodils as a centrepiece, very pale-green pillar candles (not to be confused with the deep-green candles that adorn the table on St Patrick's Day), silver cutlery, crystal glassware (obviously my mother's influence). To eat, roast lamb dotted with garlic and rosemary and cooked on sliced garlicky creamy potatoes, ratatouille and honey-coated carrots, all followed by a nice gooey dessert. And lots of chocolate! Those Easter celebrations took a lot of preparation and my memory of the end of those days is of collapsing into the armchair and putting my feet up on the coffee table, hoping there was no melted chocolate in the vicinity! It was all worth it, though.

I am just hardwired for those kind of gatherings. I am at my happiest when I am organising, planning, making memories for family and friends. I have no doubt that those happy times spent together keep us all connected in a very real way and help us to genuinely care for each other in good times and bad. That, for me, is the essence of good living and at the core of what matters for me in life.

In later years, we have spent some wonderful family Easters on the Aran Islands in my sister Deirdre's house. We would arrive en masse, laden with food: Rachel Allen's delicious smoked salmon, leek and potato pie for Good Friday, luscious, creamy lasagne from the Avoca cookbook for Saturday, gallons of Neven Maguire's roast tomato and red pepper soup to keep us fortified during the days, especially after a brisk walk, and, of course, industrial quantities of chocolate for the season that was in it. Deirdre would have scones and brown bread baked and desserts aplenty. There was no fear of us ever going hungry.

There is something very comforting and wholesome about a table heaving under good food, prepared by different members of a group for all to share, a display of affection and love and a good indicator of the things that matter in life, occasions that bring us ever closer together. Easter on Inis Mór would include us all going to the Easter vigil where the Paschal fire would be lit outside the darkened church into which the light would eventually return with the announcement of the resurrection. Lovely symbolism and a meaningful way to celebrate Easter.

Easter was different this year. The decorations were dotted around the house in the lead up to the big day but the house was empty for the holiday weekend. As happened on Valentine's Day, my brood spent Easter with their partners, taking advantage of the long weekend to get out of the city. Don't go reaching for the tissues on my behalf, though. I was delighted for them. And I was away, too, in New York, my first time to celebrate Easter in the Big Apple. I went there with a teacher friend, Betty, her first trip ever to the States. We had a wonderful time. The journey there was a bit of a disappointment, though.

I am a great supporter of our Irish companies and institutions. Aer Lingus is one that I have always held in very high regard. When I see the shamrock on the tail of the plane and am greeted by the cabin crew in their green and blue uniforms, I feel comfortable and quite proud.

It's a number of years since I travelled on a long-haul flight with Aer Lingus. In recent years, visiting Korea and various countries in Africa, it's been, of necessity, with other airlines. I was really looking forward to this Aer Lingus flight but I was quite surprised by how things have changed in the past few years. The cabin crew were as friendly and helpful as ever, the flight was smooth and the pilots kept passengers well informed of our progress. But where it fell down for me was the level of hospitality. Traditionally, you could be assured of a certain level of food and drink on a long-haul flight, and while I'm quite happy to pay for my tea and coffee on short flights, trans-Atlantic is different. Food is the time-honoured way of making people feel welcome and special. Call me old fashioned but I was surprised that there was no meat-free choice on Good Friday of all days. No dessert. No mint for the *cupán tae*. If you wanted a glass of wine with your meal, you paid for it. When did this all change? No doubt it has to do with the downturn and cutbacks, but I expected more of a *céad míle fáilte* and felt disappointed that my beloved Aer Lingus had reached this stage. Thankfully, though, the staff as ever were first-class which went a long way way towards compensating for the lack of frills.

The Irish hospitality that was in short supply on the flight to New York was in contrast to the *fáilte fial* that awaited Betty and me as we entered the arrivals hall at JFK. There to meet us was our host for the Easter weekend, a Kerryman who's been living and working in New York for almost thirty years now. We stayed in the home he shares with his partner, a New Yorker, outside the city and they told us we were now in our granny's! They couldn't have been more welcoming if they'd tried.

We went on a drive around Harlem, stopping for photos outside the Apollo Theatre, which has certainly lived up to its motto, 'where stars are born and legends are made', having launched the careers of so many African-American stars, like Billie Holiday, Stevie Wonder and Sammy Davis Jr. Ella Fitzgerald's career began when she entered an amateur talent contest at the Apollo at the age of seventeen. She was actually supposed to do a dance routine but was overawed by a dance duo who performed before her so she decided to sing instead. Ella won the talent contest and the top prize of twenty-five dollars, and the rest is history. We have the dancing Edwards Sisters to thank for the wonderful singer that was Ella Fitzgerald. Martin Luther King Day is celebrated there every year, the theatre echoing the lines of his 'I Have a Dream' speech, delivered in front of the Lincoln Centre in Washington in August 1963:

'I have a dream that one day this nation will rise up and live out the true meaning of its creed: We hold these truths to be self evident: that all men are created equal.'

We visited the oldest surviving building in New York, Fraunces Tavern, which was built in 1719 as a townhouse for the DeLancey family. It became the headquarters for the founding fathers and the Sons of Liberty under George Washington. The tavern now houses a museum of the period as well as serving good food in very cosy surroundings, including a real fire. Oh, and did I mention that it's owned and run by three Irish people? We're everywhere.

Easter Sunday began with mass in the Church of St Anne, the local parish church, which was packed – it is every Sunday – with children, teenagers, families and older people. In a word, all generations. The choir sang, the congregation answered the prayers and the church looked beautiful, bedecked as it was with hundreds of lilies, cherry blossoms and forsythia in giant tubs, a very good illustration of Easter as described by the American Christian writer, Samuel Dickey Gordon:

'Easter spells out beauty, the rare beauty of new life.'

There was an atmosphere of joy, of celebration, of belonging, of pride in their church, sentiments that have become faded and diminished back home over the past few years. I know there is a good turnout for Easter mass and Christmas mass in Ireland but on other Sundays, you can forget it and you can particularly forget the young-adult sector.

At weddings in Ireland in recent years, I've noticed that the priest actually directs the congregation from the altar as to when they should stand, kneel or sit. The answers to the prayers are barely audible because people don't know them and don't know what to do when. Not so the people in St Anne's, New York on Easter Sunday. The impression I got was that they wanted to be there. They answered out loud and proud. Their faith matters to them, punctuates their lives, has meaning for them.

I wondered why this atmosphere is practically non-existent in Ireland. I know we've had our history of despicable abuses in the Church – but so have the Americans. I think we are just a bit lazy about our religion. The majority of people who don't rise themselves to go to mass on Sundays still want to be married in and buried from the church. We have a very laissez-faire attitude, which is a pity, really, because the community that goes with the local church can only thrive with active participation. I tell you, it's energetic, vibrant and welcoming in New York State. A fraction of the enthusiasm that I witnessed on Easter Sunday would go down well back home.

After mass, we made our way back to the house to prepare Easter lunch for the eleven people whom our hosts had invited to meet the two Irish visitors and help celebrate the day. This was a lovely occasion. The table was elegantly set with a starched white tablecloth and napkins, ornate cutlery, crystal glassware, white candles and a vase of canna lilies in the centre. The leg of lamb was prepared with garlic and rosemary and sprinkled with brandy, seasoned and put in the oven to roast before being served with mashed and roast potatoes, carrots and parsnips. That was the main course on a tasty and lavish menu. There were canapés when the guests arrived. The starter was chicken liver pâté served on a bed of endives and it was followed by a delicious home-made fish soup. Then there was a salad, the main course and a selection of desserts: apple cobbler, cheesecake, fruit chocolate cups. A great celebration of Easter, a very convivial occasion with lots of chat and lots of laughs, a wonderful and genuine display of hospitality on the part of our hosts, a loving couple who entertained their guests with warmth, love and generosity.

This loving couple also happens to be a gay couple and they are an excellent example of what matters in life – warmth, love, friendship and fun. They work hard, they have a comfortable home, good friends – they enjoy life. They are in their fifties so both of them grew up in situations where it was difficult to be gay, the American partner probably less restricted in his youth than the Kerryman, who grew up in a country where homosexuality was a crime until David Norris took the state to the European Court of Human Rights in 1988, having lost the case he took against the Attorney General in the High Court and the appeal he took to the Supreme Court.

The decriminalisation of homosexuality was finally written into Irish law in 1993, which means that gay people of a certain age, like my friend from Kerry, grew up being told that the way they felt was wrong, sinful and that they had to be - and could be - cured. As parents, we try so hard to develop a sense of confidence and self-esteem in our children. We want them to grow up happy, self-assured, able to stand up for themselves and for what they believe. Can you imagine what it was like for my friend's mother and father as they reared their young son in an atmosphere of denial, at best, or hatred, at worst, towards homosexuality. They must have felt helpless, frightened for him, scared of what lay ahead for him. That's if they were even aware of his sexual orientation.

Can you imagine what it was like for him realising he was gay in a country where it was a sin and a crime, feeling, like his parents, helpless and frightened for the future? It makes me so angry to think that such a situation prevailed in my country until as recently as 1993. All of my children were born before the law changed - that's how recent we're talking about. It is abhorrent to me that a whole sector of our brothers and sisters were criminalised instead of being nurtured into healthy sexuality as they went from childhood to puberty, to adolescence and adulthood.

Thankfully, and at long last, that situation has changed. Look at all the happy couples that have celebrated civil unions since January 2011 when they became legal. And I look forward to celebrating lots of marriages with my gay friends with the same excitement and emotionally charged anticipation as when I celebrate with heterosexual friends now that the law on civil marriage is changing, too. It saddens and angers me to think that generations of Irish men and women were denied their human and civil right to happiness and a sense of ease in their relationships because of their sexual orientation.

Katherine Lee Bates is best known as the American songwriter and poet who wrote the words to the anthem 'America the Beautiful'. Katherine wrote beautifully about Easter and I think her words are particularly apt as we celebrate that time of hope and renewal and as we discuss the new reality of marriage equality for all in Ireland:

'It is the hour to rend thy chains,
The blossom time of souls.'

It gladdens me to report that my friend from Kerry is happy and successful in his personal and his professional life, is a devout Catholic, a kind and compassionate man, always looking out for people in need. And, by the way, he and his partner got married a few years ago. A wonderful celebration, attended by his elderly father and all the family. I have no doubt that his late mother was smiling down on him from above, with love in her heart and perhaps a tear in her eye.

For my part, as I enter into a new decade of living, my enjoyment of Easter will continue. There is something very special about this time of the year, a sense of light, of hope, of renewal. I will treasure the memories of family celebrations around my kitchen table and those on our western shores for the joy and the sense of belonging that they afforded me and my family. I will also treasure the memory of Easter 2015 in New York, and the insight it gave me into the universal truth that love and commitment are what matter in relationships and that everybody on this earth has a right to enjoy that. Yes indeed, a time of light and hope and renewal.

'Pull up a chair.
Take a taste.
Come join us.
Life is so endlessly delicious.'

Ruth Reichl

7.

Food, Friendship and Fighting the Flab

'Food, in the end, in our own tradition,
is something holy. It's not about nutrients
and calories. It's about sharing.
It's about honesty. It's about identity.'

Louise Fresco

The words above belong to the Dutch scientist Louise Fresco, whose passion is food sustainability. I admire her recognition that food is something that unites us, reminds us that we are part of a family or a group of friends, a community. Food brings out the best in us. Cooking for somebody is an act of caring, an act of love. Eating with people is an act of belonging, of entering into the group.

It's no secret that I love cooking for people. I like to have people gather in my home, relax and have food. It's always very informal, simple fare and an opportunity for a good chat, a catch-up and a few laughs. I also love going to other people's homes and having a meal. I appreciate the effort people make to invite friends, to cook for them, to want to share their company. I enjoy the food but for me the most important part is the company.

'If you really want to make a friend,
go to someone's house and eat with him …
people who give you their food
give you their heart.'
Cesar Chavez

Somebody who very definitely gives his heart when it comes to food and cooking is Neven Maguire, well known as the chef and owner of McNean House in the tiny village of Blacklion in County Cavan. He has singlehandedly put Blacklion on the map and the restaurant is renowned for its delicious and imaginative food, its warm welcome and the fact that you've got to book well in advance to get a table.

The culinary highlight of my year, without a shadow of a doubt, was the day I cooked for Neven – in my kitchen! His RTÉ cookery programmes are ratings winners and when he asked me to cook something for him in my kitchen as part of his latest series, I was chuffed. And petrified! Neven and I go back a long way. His first appearance on television was on *Open House* with Marty Whelan and yours truly back in 1999. His star quality shone so brightly that he very quickly became our resident chef and his cookery slot every Tuesday was eagerly anticipated by the viewers and also by my children. Neven is one of the most generous people I know and every week he would bring in an extra batch of whatever he was going to cook and give it to me to bring home for the dinner. My children's parting shot to me on a Tuesday morning as I dropped them to school on the way into RTÉ was, 'What's Neven cooking today?' They knew they were in for a treat for dinner that night.

Open House finished up in 2004 but my friendship with Neven has endured. Marty, his wife Maria, my daughter Eva and I had a wonderful time at his wedding to Amelda. I cried tears of joy when they welcomed their gorgeous twins, Connor and Lucia, into the world. I cried tears of sadness when Neven's mother and mentor Vera died, and I burst with pride when I hear of another award or another initiative at the restaurant. He is a dear friend.

I wanted everything to be just so for the day's filming at the house. I went into planning mode. Timing was key. There was a countdown. Garden cleared and flowers planted: four weeks in advance. Conservatory spring cleaned: two weeks in advance. Friend's garden furniture and lanterns borrowed and positioned on the decking: one week in advance. Decking hoovered: three days in advance. (I kid you not. I hoovered the decking to get rid of all the little bits of soil that might have lodged in between the planks. There is a photo to prove it!) Windows cleaned and grass cut: two days in advance. Flowers bought and placed in vases: one day in advance. All ready for the off.

You may be forgiven for thinking that my focus was slightly off the point. We were filming a cookery segment after all. For me, though, the house and the garden had to be right or I wouldn't feel comfortable and I have to say Neven and the camera crew were impressed. So much so that instead of his walking up to the front door at the beginning of the piece, he came around the back and walked through the colourful garden.

I'd say the director was less impressed by the fact that I had invited a few (ten, to be precise) foodie friends and family to watch Neven. I'm sure he was nervous that they would make noise or move about. He needn't have worried. I had them well briefed as to the need for absolute silence while we were filming and there was, quite simply, no room for them to move around. My kitchen is not big and there were two cameramen, two sound engineers, all their equipment, the director, Neven and me installed already so it was a tight squeeze but no one complained. Neven was, as always, genuinely charming with everyone, the food got cooked and the pals got fed. Not only that, but the director included them in the final shots, eating what I had cooked and saying it was tasty. Result!

I suppose you're interested to know what I cooked for this multiple award-winning maestro who has a real gift and passion for good food and has fine-tuned his skills at Michelin-starred restaurants all around the world. I cooked beef in Guinness and mashed potato. And he loved it. I spent ages trying to decide what to cook. I looked up books and I watched some earlier episodes of Neven's programmes. I asked family and friends for suggestions and I finally decided that I should cook as I normally do when I'm having people to dinner.

People who know me understand that for me it's about the gathering, the chat, the laughs. I always serve something that can be prepared in advance. I couldn't bear the stress of sweating over a hot stove when everybody is sitting at the table, so I favour the one-pot wonders. I love spag bol and lasagne, which are classics, Neven has lovely recipes for chicken korma and fish pie, Rachel Allen does a great smoked salmon, leek and potato gratin and, if I say so myself, my beef in Guinness is not too shabby! It's an amalgam, if you please, of two recipes, one from Avoca and the other from Brenda Costigan's cookery columns of years ago. As my grandfather and my uncle had worked as labourers in the vat room at Guinness, I thought it would be nice to remember that family heritage on this special occasion.

I had everything ready for Neven and the crew when they arrived. It's not all about flowers and clean windows, you know! It's about sharp knives – Neven had to sharpen mine before he started – and lots of clean tea towels. Panic stations. I had clean towels but they had come off the loser in the washing machine on occasion when pitted against the strength of coloured items. No shortage of clean pinkish or greyish or blueish towels. I rummaged in the hot press and pulled out a few souvenir ones from various holiday locations that are irresistible when you're abroad but seem a bit kitsch when you produce them under the grey Irish skies that we're used to. There was also a very pretty tea towel adorned with cupcakes and a logo that summed up my life thus far: 'I'll diet tomorrow!'

The cooking went well. Neven chopped carrots, I sweated onions and the audience was in awe of this man's ease and flair around food. We reminisced about *Open House*, the laughs with Marty, the camera crews who loved working on Tuesdays because we all got to taste what Neven had cooked when the programme went off air, and we talked about the loves of his life, the twins and Amelda.

When it came to putting the casserole in the oven, Neven was impressed by how clean it was. I told a white lie – I said I'd had cleaned it specially for him. Well, I had given it a rub of a cloth. That's all it needed because it was brand new. There is no way I would have allowed Neven near the oven that was in my kitchen up to the previous week. It was ancient and owed us nothing. When the oven was on, the kitchen was like a sauna, and we're not talking about an Aga here. The fan was as loud as a jet engine. And the grill was broken. For two years, my family had baked sausages and rashers at the weekends. The sausages tasted okay; the rashers resembled cardboard. Neven's visit was timely therefore. We now have a silent, sealed, squeaky-clean fan oven, which positively gleamed on the telly. And the following

Saturday everyone was up early for a long-forgotten treat: a few grilled rashers and sausages for breakfast.

If anyone ever needs reminding, that day cooking for Neven would be a wonderful example of what matters in life. This is a man who is highly regarded here in Ireland and internationally as a master of his craft; he creates truly imaginative and inspirational dishes: combinations like turbot with crab cannelloni and prawn velouté or vanilla crème brulée with poached apple compote trip off his tongue. He runs an award-winning restaurant, has written several cookery books and has made many successful cookery programmes for television. He is an artist and yet, on that day when the food was wholesome but ordinary, he was as enthusiastic as if I had rustled up an assiette of rare-breed pork comprising caramelised belly, smoked bacon-wrapped fillet and pork and leek sausage. And pigs might fly (with respect to that pork dish, one of Neven's specialities)! Neven was delighted to be there, he valued what I was cooking and he loved the fact that my friends and family were there to enjoy it too. He realises that the real joy of life is in human interaction and that food has a part to play in that.

'Eating is not merely a material pleasure. Eating well gives a spectacular joy to life and contributes immensely to goodwill and happy companionship. It is of great importance to the morale.'

Elsa Schiaparelli

There was a lot of happy companionship in my kitchen that day, reminiscing with Neven about good times on *Open House*, introducing my friends and family to this master chef and getting the dish cooked and eaten. Ordinary as it is, I offer you, in all humility, my take on beef in Guinness:

500 ml Guinness (*very important!*)

1 tbsp French mustard (*nothing insular about this dish*)

sprig of fresh rosemary (*I grow my own, don't you know!*)

2 bay leaves

1 kg cubed lean stewing beef (*Irish*)

2 onions (*handy household tip: wear goggles when peeling them – the only people crying, with laughter, will be the people who see you wearing them*)

2 cloves of garlic, chopped

3 carrots, diced

3 stalks of celery, chopped

175 g button mushrooms, halved

425 ml beef stock, made with a cube (*easy peasy*)

25 g butter

4 tbsp olive oil

1 tbsp flour

1 tsp redcurrant jelly (*I use half a jar – a teaspoon is nothing*)

2 tsp tomato purée (*that's enough of that*)

salt and freshly ground pepper (*everyone knows that*)

You marinade the beef in half the can of Guinness, the mustard, the rosemary and bay leaves overnight. Then remove it from the marinade and fry it in batches in the oil and transfer it to a casserole dish. Fry the onion and garlic and add them to the casserole. Fry the mushrooms in the butter. Add the flour to them then and make a paste. Pour in the stock and transfer all that to the casserole. Pour in the marinade and the rest of the Guinness, unless it's 'gone'. Add the carrots, celery, salt, pepper, tomato purée and redcurrant jelly and bring the whole lot to the boil before covering and cooking at 170°C for about two hours, until the meat is tender.

I'm not going to insult anybody's intelligence by giving a recipe for mashed potato. Everybody has their own way of doing it. Mine involves lots of butter and a certain amount of cream. That's another reason why I'm not giving the recipe! As Neven says: 'Happy Cooking.'

Perhaps this might be a good time to mention a less pleasurable aspect of food: the dreaded weight gain and the elusive weight loss. This is a subject close to my heart, particularly today for reasons I shall disclose very shortly.

I know I am not huge but I have been overweight and I put on the extra pounds very easily. I watch what I eat and I make the effort to diet and exercise because I am not happy when my clothes are tight on me.

There are times of the year when I address this issue and I have been on a roll of eating the correct food and exercising and enjoying the results. I am, however, only human and, guess what? I fell off the wagon last night. But ... today is the first day of the rest of my life. Again!

I have said this before on so many occasions I have lost count. This time, I'm very disappointed, though. I feel a bit hard done by. I couldn't sleep last night. I just tossed and turned trying to figure out where I had gone wrong, what had happened to the plan.

All I could think about was the disappointment and the fact that I thought I was doing so well. And I was. But you know what they say. The scales do not lie. I stood up on them in the community centre and before I could make out the numbers, I could tell from the look on Deirdre the leader's face that it was not good news. I had gained two and a half pounds in a week. Devastation. Any woman or man who has gone down the weight-loss route will understand what I'm talking about. So many of us have been there. Some have a longer and a harder road to travel than others. I know I'm not massive but as one, meaning me, gets older, one finds it harder to shift the few pounds that we might gain over the Christmas or on holidays or even on a weekend away or a night out. We enjoy ourselves and then we row back and try to return to healthy eating and exercise.

You know the way children sometimes have an invisible friend. My brother John, even in middle age, has a friend like that. His name is Ned, surname Kelly, Cockney rhyming slang for belly. John's friend Ned is not always invisible, though. There are good times when, after a long, rigorous cycle perhaps, John will announce with great glee that: 'Ned is dead.' On the other hand, after Christmas or returning from holidays, we'll be informed that: 'Ned is back. He was lonely without me!' Sometimes, in an act of magnanimity and great generosity, John even brings Ned on holidays with him. Swings and roundabouts.

It's the same for us all. That's OK. I can cope with that. But I had been very careful this past week and declined lots of treats when they were offered. I had been at a wonderfully lavish birthday party in Mayo at the weekend but that made me even more determined to refuse any biscuits or other treats when I returned to Dublin.

I was in recovery mode for the weigh-in – for all the world like a boxer trying to make the weight before a fight. Maybe, like a boxer, I was a bit cocky as well. A few months ago I had stood on the scales in fear and trepidation, having returned from ten fabulous days in

New York, eating and drinking my way around the city that never sleeps, and I had gained no weight. I couldn't believe it. I was delighted. Now I had walked the length and breadth of Manhattan during those ten days so that must have stood to me, as they say. And, to be honest, I'd had no time to exercise since my return so perhaps that's the reason why I was up two and a half pounds last night. I hope so because I'm taking a trip to Portugal soon and the only weapon in my armoury will be the walking.

My friend Anita, an avid walker, is part of the group so I'll tag along with her. John is coming as well. I haven't seen him recently so I'm not sure if Ned will be joining us. We may find him over there, though. I hope Ned doesn't have a sister that is looking for a new friend. I hate to be rude but I do not want to allow her into my life. It's a question of pride as well, in a way, because I have reached my healthy goal weight and have a gold card and I certainly do not want to lose that. It's been an up-and-down struggle and I was delighted to have arrived at this point. It's nice not to feel that you're 'bet' into a pair of jeans or a dress. I no longer avoid waisted 'garments', as the nuns used to refer to them in our domestic science classes years ago. I am determined. Again. Onwards and upwards.

I never tire of hearing other people's stories of struggles with weight. I can relate to every one of them. Let's face it, food is something we all have in common. We cannot live without it. It provides fuel, nourishment, comfort and pleasure, depending on the circumstance. Food is at the centre of celebrations and family gatherings. Is there anything nicer than cooking a meal for a friend? Well, yes. Being invited to put your feet up while a friend cooks for you!

There's no doubt we have a fascination with health and food. We all know the theory, the foods that fuel our bodies and enhance our health and well being. We know about the sugary foods that lead to cravings, weight gain and sluggishness. The American triathlete and writer Sally Edwards puts it up to us when she says:

> 'If we're not willing to settle for junk living, we certainly shouldn't settle for junk food.'

There is a real problem with obesity in the western world and sugar and carbohydrate intake is a main cause. We are well informed by *Operation Transformation* on RTÉ television every year about the risks we expose ourselves to when we ignore the warnings about healthy eating. The programme has been a phenomenal success and has transformed many lives for the better. It comes into our sitting rooms at a very good time of the year, January, when we are full of good intentions and resolve and the team leaders certainly motivate their followers all around the country to get fit and lose weight.

It's a must-see in my house, along with *Grey's Anatomy*. Eva and I have a rule that neither of us is allowed to watch either programme unless the other person is present. Thank goodness for Sky+. Sometimes, we have an *Operation Transformation* feast, although it's probably a bit insensitive to use that word to describe a couple of programmes watched one after the other.

I have great admiration for the leaders as they embark on a totally new way of living. It's tough. We all know how hard it is to break a habit. These brave people do just that: they bite the bullet and transform their lives. And they transform the lives of many people who follow them during the eight weeks of *Operation Transformation*. We see them out training in all sorts of awful weather and we will them on – from the comfort of our armchairs, admittedly. We watch as they weigh their food and discover new tastes and flavours that, in a lot of cases, they would have turned their noses up at before. We feel their pain and want to give them a hug when they don't lose as much as they should in any given week, particularly if they incur the wrath of one of the mentors. And we holler and cheer and say, 'Wow', when they emerge onto the catwalk in the final programme, in new clothes that are several sizes smaller than they would have contemplated previously.

The stories of the leaders strike a chord with any of us who have put on a few pounds and seen them become more than a few and who have, over time, lost heart and thrown our hat at it and just gone and bought the next size up when shopping for clothes. It happens so easily and yet, on the other hand, it most definitely doesn't happen so easily when we decide, 'That's it. I'm going to lose that extra weight.' No, siree! It's hard work and it gets harder as we get older. Trust me. I know this. I've been there. And of course losing the flab is not the end of the story. The difficulty is maintaining the momentum and deciding that this is the new me. Or that this is the first day of the rest of my life, like today is for me. Again.

A group of people for whom I have great regard are the ones who decide their weight has gone past the healthy point, lose the surplus once and once only, and that's it for life. Do they exist? Yes, they do. Their DNA includes self-control and discipline in amounts that I marvel at and am unfamiliar with in my own make-up. I wonder, though, has the joy gone out of food for such people. For me, food is quite simply one of life's pleasures. The problem is that it's always on my mind. I'm either delighted with myself because I have foregone that pleasure or I'm disgusted with myself because, once again, I have thrown caution to the wind and persuaded myself that life is short and what the hell! I wonder sometimes could I even spell discipline and control. Not my strong points, I'm afraid. Don't get me wrong. I can do the straight and narrow. But when I'm on that path, I'm constantly thinking about food and what I'm missing. I'm being good, though. And isn't that what counts?

There's another thing. The vocabulary that we use around weight loss needs a bit of examination. I'm 'good' if I have denied myself lots of different foods. I've had a 'good week' if I've eaten meals that are plain and without the embellishments of sauces, oils or, heaven forbid, mayonnaise. I've had a bad week if the opposite is true. I'm either on the straight and narrow or I have fallen off the wagon. My daughter has a pet name for our weight-loss class: Fat Club! We definitely need to evaluate the language we use around weight loss. It's all about sacrifice, it seems. Not a good mindset to have when I'm wanting to lose the few pounds. But I do it and it works to an extent.

I should clarify here that I'm not talking about skinny minnies. I quite simply do not think an enforced super-slim size zero is attractive. It's fine for people who have the skeletal framework to match it but I hate the size-zero mentality. A friend of mine and one of Ireland's creative geniuses, Don O'Neill, agrees. He is a highly talented fashion designer from Ballyheigue in Kerry, a place of great coastal beauty that has inspired some of his intricately crafted beaded gowns that replicate the sun shimmering on the sea outside the bed and breakfast where he grew up.

Don spent time honing his talents in the studio of Christian Lacroix in Paris before moving to New York where he now has his own label. He designs for all the big names in the movie and TV world, people like Taylor Swift, Carrie Underwood, Oprah Winfrey and Khloé Kardashian. I admire Don's philosophy that celebrates the female form in its different shapes and sizes. Before 2014's Oscars, he came to the rescue of Gabourey Sidibe, a very large young woman who has been in many TV shows and who was nominated for an Oscar in her debut movie *Precious*. Some designers were reluctant to dress Gabourey for the awards ceremony because of her size, feeling she wouldn't be a good advertisement for their product. Don O'Neill was not one of them and he offered to design a dress for her. She looked stunning, confident and beautiful as she graced the red carpet in her shocking-pink floor-length Theia gown. Well done, Gabourey. Well done, Don.

At this stage of my life, I accept totally that my body shape has changed. I still want to be fit and healthy, though, and there is nothing to compare with pulling up a zip on a dress and feeling a little bit of wriggle room, hence this latest bout of healthy eating and exercise and the decision that I am going to be weighed each week. It's so easy to fall off the wagon, though, and down the slippery slope to old habits and a reversal of all the good work.

When I arrived home from the community centre last night, I gave vent to my disappointment by buttering several slices of crusty white bread and eating them. After my dinner. This, of course, added to my disappointment and transferred that disappointment from the weight gain, a cruel interloper and a third party, to little aul' me for my lack of will power. Under the circumstances, 'little' is probably not the best adjective to use to describe myself.

As well as adding to my disappointment, that crusty buttery bread no doubt added another pound or two to the tally. I will definitely be pounding those pavements in Portugal on my holiday. I hope the weather is really hot so that I can sweat off a few extra ounces with the heat. Like a boxer again. I'll be fighting fit when I get home. That's the plan, anyway.

It's important to have a plan: it gives a project structure and a yardstick by which to measure progress. For me, the plan has become a bit unstuck. I need to be watchful of what I eat. I don't feel good about myself when I'm overindulging. It matters to me to be fit and healthy. You can imagine how I feel, therefore, admitting to the bread and butter binge last night. It's time to refocus and to be positive and to fight the good fight!

There's been quite a focus on healthy eating in my family in recent times. When Lucy settled in Korea two years ago she took a long hard look at her diet and decided to eliminate gluten and dairy. A short while later, she cut out meat and fish and then decided to adopt a vegan diet and lifestyle. She eats nothing that is in any way animal based. There is a philosophy of care for animal life that is central to this and it extends to other areas besides food. No woollen jumper, no leather shoes or bags, no silk scarves. You're right: Christmas and birthdays are a nightmare now. What do you buy the person who wants none of the things we are so used to giving as gifts?

Lucy did a lot of research before embarking on veganism, which has now become a way of life for her. I admire her passion and her commitment, and I could have done with a bit of her self-discipline last night.

When she was living in Korea, the food possibilities were limited due to lack of supply. Now that she's in

Australia, the world is her oyster. Wrong analogy. She wouldn't eat oysters. She is spoilt for choice, though, when it comes to alternatives for some of the staples that we take for granted. She eats gluten-free, dairy-free bread, vegan cheeses and chocolate and while we were Skyping recently she showed me the gluten-free vegan pizza she and her flatmate had ordered after a hard day's work. It looked amazing – good enough to eat indeed!

Lucy is sharing an apartment with a friend from home who has gone vegan since Lucy joined her from Korea. I hope her mother is pleased! It's certainly suiting Lucy. She positively glows with healthy skin, bright eyes and shiny hair. Her digestive system is well balanced, she has bundles of energy and she sleeps better than she ever did. She did take after her mother regarding sleep, or lack of same.

Insomnia and me are bedfellows, literally. During the day, if exhaustion hits me while I'm driving I can pull over and catnap in the car. I can doze off in an armchair, but lie me down in a comfy bed on a soft pillow and the sandman legs it out the window and the ceiling listens to my woes as I try to sleep but don't.

Why, I hear you ask, do I not try the vegan solution myself? Because it's hard, hard work. I suppose it gets easier as time goes on, but one of my memories of last Christmas is of going from shop to shop sourcing ingredients that would sit well with a vegan. I cooked a few dishes for Lucy while she was at home for the holidays but they weren't hugely successful. First attempts rarely are, and with vegan dishes the consistency is different so that takes getting used to as well. I'm very proud, though, of the vegan brownies I made at Christmas. Lucy loved them. In case you'd like to give them a go here's the recipe.

150 g hazelnuts
150 g Medjool dates, stoned
Small pinch of salt
50 g raw cacao powder
3 tsp coconut oil

You blend the hazelnuts for about three minutes in the food processor or a blender, then add in the dates, salt and cacao powder. Slowly add the coconut oil as the mixture is blending. When it's nicely mushed together, use a spatula to scrape the mixture onto a baking tray. Put it in the freezer for a half hour and then leave it in the fridge until you want to serve it.

You have to put your expectations of brownies as we know them to one side for this, and allow your tastebuds to engage with these new sensations. In other words, if you're expecting them to taste like brownies, you'll be disappointed. We are used to far too many refined sugars. Vegans get their sweetness for the most part from fruits like dates. I've seen Lucy cook dishes using bananas in place of eggs and she made a very nice chocolate mousse when she was home last Christmas using mashed avocado. It was delicious.

In other dietary news, my son Tom decided to go the Paleo route a few months ago. That's the caveman diet, favoured by Gwyneth Paltrow and others. You eat totally non-processed foods. He studied a book written by a friend of his from Galway, *Naked Paleo* – that's the name of the book, not a reference to Tom's friend. Then he started doing the necessary shopping and set about cooking. I was astounded when I saw Tom preparing his breakfast. Piles of food like spinach, kale, olives, feta cheese, cashew nuts, raisins all atop an omelette. Alongside that, porridge made up of flaxseed, coconut milk, ground almonds with blueberries on the top and to wash it all down a smoothie which is full of good things and quite tasty. This is how it goes:

225 ml almond milk
120 g blueberries
1 tbsp chia seeds
1 tsp maple syrup
Half a ripe avocado
Pinch of cinnamon

Put everything in a blender and whizz well. I have tasted this smoothie and it's delicious.

Tom has always been a good eater but I have never seen him put away so much food as he has since taking up Paleo. The upshot of this new regimen is that he has lost eight pounds. Now I know that if I or any of my friends, acquaintances or enemies even lost eight pounds we would be doing cartwheels around the kitchen. Not so Tom. He didn't want to lose weight and was on the verge of chucking the whole thing in. He didn't, though, and he, like his sister, is in rude good health, fit as a fiddle, energetic and sleeping like a log. Mind you, like most men, Tom never really had a problem in that department. But all this well being is because of eating non-processed high-fibre foods.

This talk of food and eating has made me decidedly hungry. I think it's time I treated myself to a bit of a snack. A healthy snack, of course. I'll leave the last words about food to the late Luciano Pavarotti, who enjoyed the good things in life, including the joys of the table:

> *'One of the very nicest things about life is the way we must regularly stop whatever it is we are doing and devote our attention to eating.'*

I couldn't agree more!

'Love and compassion are
necessities, not luxuries.
Without them humanity
cannot survive.'

Dalai Lama

8.

Living the Christian Message

'I like your Christ. I do not like your Christians.
Your Christians are so unlike your Christ.'

Mahatma Gandhi

We need to talk about ... Jesus, just as Kevin's family needed to talk about Kevin in the novel by Lionel Shriver. Jesus is, for Christians, at the centre of our lives as Kevin was the pivot of his family's life. The problem is that, as in Kevin's case, things have gone sadly wrong. What matters for Christians is the Christian message that centres around loving God and loving our neighbour. If we follow those guidelines, we won't go far wrong. In fact, we can do a lot that's right and good. Sometimes, however, Jesus is sidelined in Christian lives, even in situations of religious observance, and there are occasions when it's the priest, Jesus' representative among us, who behaves in a way that I feel would be alien to Jesus. I'm not talking about the well-documented cases of clerical abuse which, as well as being un-Christlike, are criminal acts and need to be punished just like any other crime. But Jesus and what he stands for can seem to take a back seat when a feeling of self-importance and entitlement emanates from the man wearing the vestments and celebrating the mass.

I came across a good example of this in spring 2015 in Portugal during a week's holiday with family and friends. We arrived on Saturday evening and settled in to a cosy, welcoming environment in a friend's villa, which had been lent to us for a week. Everything was perfect from the get-go. There were six of us. We travelled Ryanair and the fact that we were allocated seats on the flight was the equivalent of an Aer Lingus upgrade, when you turn left into business class as you enter the aircraft, feeling very posh and a little bit special. No scuffling or jockeying for position required. It was heaven. The next morning we spent a very convivial few hours drinking tea and eating toast by the pool, marvelling at the feeling of heat at such an ungodly hour on our pale Irish skin.

We relaxed into an easy rhythm that set the tone for the week. These days, we tend to work very hard – increasingly long hours in increasingly pressurised environments. If that pressure is not released and balanced with relaxation and time spent with people we care about, it can become oppressive. A woman I admire greatly and who is a dynamo of energy and ambition is Hillary Clinton. Nobody could ever accuse her of giving less than 100 per cent to any project she has embraced throughout her life, be it politics, the presidency, the law, women's rights, marriage, family. Her words make a lot of sense:

'Never confuse having a career with having a life.'

That week in Portugal was an opportunity to put work to one side and focus on having a life, chatting, laughing and catching up. This is something that matters hugely to me. We all have periods in our lives when we have no time to ourselves. I felt like that when my children were small and needed my attention and, as they got older, my chauffeuring skills. When I look back on those days, I had time then to play the piano in the evening, to read books in the afternoon, to paint my nails and wait for them to dry. I can't remember the last time I enjoyed any of those pursuits. I honestly feel we are inclined to fill our days with more and more *doing* to the detriment of just *being*. The inclination is to keep busy, be on the go the whole time. Even leisure time is all about doing. The Roman poet Ovid, who lived in the fifth century BC, gave sound advice when he said:

'Take rest; a field that has rested gives a bountiful crop.'

I cannot imagine what Ovid would think of present-day mores where so many of us feel there aren't enough hours in the day. There were plenty of hours in the long sunny days in Portugal and it was a life-enhancing, fun and relaxing time that put the whole work–life balance question into perspective for us. I have no doubt that we could all benefit from adopting a principle of allowing ourselves to take time out. It can be in the house, in the garden, anywhere, as long as it involves a separation from the work part of our lives.

There endeth the sermon! Actually the sermon didn't end there. Back to Jesus and his place in Christian lives. As that first leisurely morning in Portugal wore on, my sister Deirdre and I decided we'd go to mass. It was different to say the least. We walked down to the church in good time for the eleven o'clock start. We could have taken our time and had another cup of tea because the mass didn't start until seventeen minutes past eleven. I checked the time when the bell gave one ring and the choir began to sing, as the priest and one server walked up the centre aisle.

The priest did not have the flustered demeanour of one who is rushing and apologetic for being late. I don't speak Portuguese but I know that *desculpe* means 'I'm sorry'. I didn't hear it. There wasn't even a *Bom dia*, 'good morning'. The first word out of the unfazed priest's mouth when he arrived on the altar and turned around to greet the congregation was '*Oremus*'. Call me old fashioned, but I think that's bad manners. He was seventeen minutes late for an eleven o'clock appointment.

I got the impression this was a regular occurrence because some members of the choir, people in the know, had been arriving into the church up to about ten past eleven. Clearly this priest had form. That form, though, is disrespectful of his congregation. There was an arrogance about the man, an air of entitlement that reminded me of priests when I was growing up. Memories came flooding into my head of my mother whipping off the tablecloth and replacing it with the good lacy one and laying out the best china when the word went round on the bush telegraph that the priest was 'making visitations' on our road. That was her way of showing respect for this man who was Christ's representative in her life.

That day has long gone in Ireland. Any priest I know would be mortified to think the *bean a' tí* was scurrying around changing tablecloths and hiding mugs as he arrived for a cuppa. I'm not so sure about this Portuguese priest, though. He had a haughty air to him. His body language was arrogant and pompous. I was incredulous that he didn't apologise for his late arrival and was just getting over my indignation, enjoying the lovely music and the people-watching, when it was time for the homily. It was long. Twenty minutes long. I know this because I timed it. This man who kept everybody waiting seventeen minutes launched into a diatribe that lasted twenty minutes. You're probably thinking I'm being unfair to the man because I don't speak Portuguese and his flock could have been hanging on his every word. I don't think so. A woman in the front row was nodding off from time to time, leaning to one side and righting herself just before she hit the seat. She was right in the priest's eyeline. Brave lady. Another woman, a member of the choir, fainted and had to be carried out of the church. I don't think it was ecstasy on her part. About fifteen minutes into the discourse, a mobile phone went off. That man got a dirty look from the altar. I was hoping it might put the priest off his stride and he might bring the homily to a close but he continued for a full five minutes more.

On the subject of the congregation, it was very different to the one that had impressed me in New York at Easter. On the positive side, the choir, made up of local men and women, was excellent. There was a lovely wooden statue of St Cecelia, the patron saint of musicians, at the back of the altar. Perhaps she inspired the choir because they sang beautifully and with great enthusiasm.

The prayers were answered out loud and clear also, as they were on Easter Sunday in New York, unlike the way they are answered in many churches in Ireland where we tend to mumble the responses. I wonder what that says about us. Have we a nonchalant attitude to mass and the clergy? Perhaps. You certainly couldn't say that about the people in this church in Portugal. Their prayers were bright and vibrant. Not so their age profile, however. I'd say Deirdre and I played our part in lowering the average age and we're not young things. The people in that church ranged from elderly to middle aged. There were no young people, no families. I know this was a holiday resort but there were schools in the town so there must have been children. Our waiter on the first evening had explained to us where the church was and told us that, in the summer, the congregation is seventy per cent Irish and thirty per cent locals. On that morning, anyone who was not local was Irish. It felt like home when we emerged from the church after mass listening to the Irish accents. There was even an Irish newspaper on sale at the shop across the road.

Walking back to the villa in the sunshine, I didn't feel I'd had an uplifting or a positive experience at that mass.

The music was enjoyable but that was all. It felt like a bit of a time warp and I asked myself if Jesus would have behaved like that priest. Would he have left people sitting waiting for him? Would he have preached at them for such a long time? Or would he have arrived on time, greeted the people with a smile that added to the lovely sunny morning, celebrated the mass, preached his homily in warm tones and thanked the congregation and the choir for their participation at the end? I go for the latter scenario, and it would be so nice if priests asked themselves more often, 'What would Jesus do in this situation?' It goes without saying that we should all use that as our reference point but in this context surely the people who have answered the call to represent Jesus and what he stood for should not lose sight of how Jesus would behave.

There are wonderful examples of a kind and loving Church that give me hope and reassurance that this religion that I include as a central part of my life is fundamentally good and worthwhile. I met Br Kevin Crowley a few years ago when he featured in a *Nationwide* programme about homeless people. He founded the Capuchin Day Centre in Dublin in 1969 because he saw homeless people coming into the church for a bit of heat and calling to the Capuchin Friary for food.

When the Day Centre opened its doors all those years ago, Br Kevin and his volunteers were providing breakfast and lunch to fifty people a day. Today, 700 people come through those doors six days a week, and are welcomed warmly and fed a nutritious cooked breakfast, and a lunch if they come back between one and three in the afternoon. The Day Centre provides showers and fresh clothes to anyone who needs them. A doctor and a nurse are there some days and the services that Br Kevin provides include chiropody, eye testing and counselling.

On one day a week, food parcels are handed out to the people as they leave, 1,600 food parcels to be precise. The Capuchin Day Centre is an oasis of caring, a sanctuary for the many hundreds of hungry, homeless people in the city of Dublin. These are people who are marginalised, perhaps through unemployment, drink or drugs. They are shunned by society. They are hopeless and helpless and vulnerable, but when they walk through the doors of the Day Centre at nine o'clock in the morning, that negativity falls away for a while because they are treated with respect and love by Br Kevin and his volunteers, who have been preparing breakfasts from the early hours. Br Kevin, the softly spoken, gentle man from Kilcolman in West Cork, is their hero. In my eyes, he is a saint. He is a man of faith, a man of love, and he is certainly doing as Jesus would in this situation. As he says himself:

'In an ideal world, I would love to see our streets free of homeless people, and everyone, especially the poor and underprivileged, treated equally with the greatest respect and dignity.'

Sadly this is not an ideal world, but Br Kevin is certainly making it a better one. His reputation has grown and encouraged others to follow in his, and therefore in Christ's, footsteps by caring for the underprivileged in their communities. In Graiguecullen in Carlow, St Clare's Hospitality began in 2013 and modelled itself on Br Kevin's centre, responding to a need for help in the area by distributing food parcels on a weekly basis. Volunteers arrive at the parish centre early in the morning to parcel up the food donated by retailers, wholesalers and individuals. They then load up their cars and bring the parcels to people who were very glad of the help.

This example of Christian living is very much a whole community project, involving the Catholic Church, Church of Ireland, Methodist and Life Churches, who would all come together in Fr John Dunphy's parish centre, roll up their sleeves and get to work.

Actually there have been a lot of rolled-up sleeves in Graiguecullen recently because they have been converting a big empty warehouse into a dining room and kitchens, again modelled on Br Kevin's set-up. This warehouse was donated by a local businessman and the fitting out was done by tradesmen who volunteered their services. It's called The Kitchen and is situated along the River Barrow. It is a place where homeless, hungry, lonely people are welcomed and invited to sit down to a hearty, nourishing meal and a chat, where they're treated with warmth and respect. It is an anchorage, a safe harbour, a sanctuary, a lifeline. Well done to the people of Graiguecullen. They have answered the call and given their time and energy on behalf of others. And it doesn't stop there.

One of the priests in the parish has donated his garden to grow vegetables for the Anchorage and a local garden centre has donated seeds and fruit trees. Again an army of volunteers rolled up to that garden to rotovate and turn the soil, ready for planting. The priest in question is Fr Liam Lawton, well known as a liturgical composer, and his words sit very nicely in this context:

> 'Even though the rain hides the stars,
> Even though the mist swirls the hills,
> Even when the dark clouds veil the sky,
> You are by my side.'

Lovely words of comfort underlining the presence of support when times are tough. It's good to know that when the lives of the vulnerable, the poor and the homeless can seem made up of darkness, rain and mist, when they feel alone and unwanted, there are people who, without judging, will provide sustenance and care to them in the name of goodness.

There are other examples of that simple living church. I have great admiration for Sr Stanislaus Kennedy, a woman of energy, charity and vision. She must be delighted with the work of people like Br Kevin and his team and St Clare's Hospitality in Carlow. It was Sr Stan who recognised the need for a charity to care for homeless people when she founded Focus Ireland back in 1985. Mind you, the fact that there is still a huge problem with homelessness in our cities and towns is a source of frustration and sadness to her today.

Sr Stan has always worked on behalf of the disadvantaged. She set up the Immigrant Council of Ireland in 2001 to reflect our changing society and to provide support to people coming to settle in this country. Although Sr Stan is in her seventies, she's still active and one of her ongoing projects is the Young Social Innovators programme which sees transition-year students from all over the country embark on projects of social significance. The students choose a topic and enter their project in different categories. The headings for these categories always begin with the words 'Making Our World Better ...' They cover every aspect of life from mental health to physical well being, to social inclusion and poverty eradication, to green living and justice for all. As President Higgins, patron of YSI, said:

> 'At the heart of Young Social Innovators is the dvelopment of active, creative citizens. And it is active, creative citizens who will lead the transformation of Ireland.'

There are now 100,000 young social innovators in this country. The ripple effect has been enormous. These young people come from every corner of Ireland, fired with enthusiasm to make this country a better place. They are outward looking and forward thinking. They care about their community and the people in it. They are aware. The overall winners for 2015 came from Largy College in Clones in County Monaghan. Their year-long project tackled discrimination against the lesbian, gay, bisexual and transgender (LGBT) community. They examined the problems of homophobia and transphobia, and their aim was to create a safe environment for LGBT students and staff in their school. Worthy winners in the year of the Equality Referendum.

You'd know Sr Stan was the person responsible for this countrywide initiative that brings more than 3,000 young people to the awards ceremony in Dublin every year. All of the categories reflect topics that have been dear to her heart since she joined the Religious Sisters of Charity in 1958 at the age of eighteen because, growing up on the Dingle Peninsula in Kerry, she always wanted to work with the poor. Sr Stan has certainly done that during the many years she has been a nun and now, in her mid-seventies, you'll find Sr Stan at the heart of the team that is intent on galvanising young people to be a force for change, a force for good in their own areas and in the wider community. I have heard Sr Stan address these transition-year students and the mantra she wants them to adopt comes from Mahatma Gandhi, with whose words I began this chapter:

'Be the change you want to see in the world.'

That's her wish for them and Sr Stan is certainly a good example of that wish. She has devoted her life to and expended all of her energies on recognising where help was needed, and has then provided it. She definitely has done what Jesus would have done in every situation in which she has found herself.

People like Sr Stan, Br Kevin and those involved in St Clare's Hospitality are just a few examples of the kind of Church I want to be a part of. Their attitude is caring; their lifestyle is simple. They are the real Church. I admire them greatly. They are the people who give me consolation and reassurance and make me want to stay involved with my Church. They understand that what matters is people, and that when it's possible to reach out and help somebody who is marginalised or vulnerable, the rewards are significant. The person feels loved and respected and that's the way it should be. Mother Teresa was right when she said:

'The poor give us much more than we give them.'

I think Jesus would be more at home with the likes of Sr Stan and Br Kevin than he would be walking along the corridors in Rome, rubbing shoulders with cardinals in flowing robes as they deliberate the way forward for the Church.

I have to say those self-same cardinals left themselves open to a lot of criticism when they embarked on a synod to discuss the family last October – 150 celibate men sitting down together to discuss what's best for you and me and our children. There wasn't a woman among them. How much more meaningful those discussions would have been had they invited women to be involved. In fact, how much better would the Church be generally if women could play a central and meaningful role.

In spring 2015, I met a very vibrant woman. She's from Iceland and she lives in Dún Laoghaire, where she has been rector for the Church of Ireland congregation of Christ Church for almost three years. Prior to that Reverend Ása Björk Ólafsdóttir was rector in Kells in County Meath, her first Irish parish since she left Reykjavik in 2010.

She trained as a teacher in Iceland when she left school but, in her mid-thirties, she felt she could no longer ignore God's calling, as she described it, so she decided she'd take a career break and study theology for a year to see if she liked it. She loved it and continued her studies for five years right up to ordination, despite the challenges of rearing three children and the breakdown of her marriage during the second year of her theology course. She is a warm, confident, compassionate human being with a religious vocation who does a very good job of caring for her flock. No sooner had she landed in Dún Laoghaire than she was looking around to see where the areas of need were. She wasn't long identifying problems of poverty, loneliness and homelessness in this fairly affluent part of south Dublin and, although she knew nothing of Br Kevin, she set up a similar facility called the Dining Room in the parish hall, where everyone is welcome to come and eat dinner three afternoons a week. Those who can afford it make a donation. Those who can't afford it are equally welcome.

On the day I visited, I met a homeless person, a man whose wife was abroad and a man who lives alone. They all sang the praises of Reverend Ása and her volunteers who quite simply make them feel special. They provide so much more than a nutritious meal to the people who come to the Dining Room. They provide company, respect and dignity, things that matter, things that can be in short supply in many vulnerable people's lives.

There's an energy about the place which is an extension of the energy that Ása exudes. She loves life and she particularly loves people. She walks the seafront on the lookout for anyone who is sitting by themselves and looking sad or lonely. She sits down beside them and has a chat. She is chaplain to the RNLI and takes an active interest in the local charity shops, some of which donate clothes to her that people can help themselves to when they visit her Dining Room. Ása is an outgoing, gregarious woman full of fun and full of reverence. She always wears her collar, even under the lovely velvet dress she was wearing the day we filmed with her for

Nationwide. She wants people to know she is a cleric and is available to provide whatever support she can. Ása is a divorced mother of three children who understands the trials of life and who has a deep religious faith which has provided her with comfort in difficult times and which she is tasked with passing on to her parishioners in Christ Church Dun Laoghaire. She also happens to have got engaged to an Irishman on her fiftieth birthday earlier this year. This is a woman of God, doing God's work happily and diligently within her Church.

There is no doubt in my mind that we could do with women like Ása in the Catholic Church. I know lots of women like her who would make wonderful priests. Wouldn't it be refreshing to feel a sense of equality in the Church that could harness the gifts and the talents of women as well as men? I don't think it's going to happen in my lifetime. Pope Francis acknowledged the special qualities of women when he said:

> 'The church acknowledges the indispensable contribution which women make to society through the sensitivity, intuition and other distinctive skill sets which they, more than men, tend to possess.

I think, for example, of the special concern which women show to others, which finds a particular, even if not exclusive, expression in motherhood.'

That's as may be. The acknowledgement doesn't go so far as to contemplate the ordination of women as well as men, which Pope Francis said 'is not a question open to discussion'.

What a shame. The Church would be a richer place if it was open to welcoming real participation by women. Maybe the way to gently open the door to women would be to allow priests to marry. We have a lot to offer! The priest I encountered in Portugal could definitely have benefited from a woman's levelling and warming touch. He might even have made it to the church on time with a smile on his face as he greeted his parishioners. It might have made Gandhi like Christians as well as Christ.

*'When we give cheerfully
and accept gratefully,
everyone is blessed.'*
Maya Angelou

9.

Turning Sixty

*'There is nothing on this earth more to
be prized than true friendship.'*

Thomas Aquinas

St Thomas Aquinas lived in the thirteenth century, a
Dominican friar and Catholic priest, an influential
philosopher and theologian whose words have lost none
of their veracity or wisdom despite the passage of more
than 800 years. Friendship is a great gift, to be treasured
and nurtured and to be enjoyed. We look out for our
friends, we offer support in times of need, we celebrate
achievements and joyous moments, we love our friends

and want the best for them. I had an unexpected reminder of the value of true friendship in September 2014.

I was really looking forward to that Saturday night. My friend's son Mike and his fiancée Anne had invited his mother Anita and me as their guests to a tasting of various menus that they were considering for their wedding reception. Anita is a wonderful cook and she's the groom's mother so it's no surprise that she was going along to help. But why me? A legitimate question, I will allow. Mike's dad, also called Michael, is a very committed member of the tennis club and he was involved in an important competition that night. A pity, really, because he too is a good cook and would have had interesting opinions on the choice of wedding menu. Anyway, one man's loss in this case was another woman's gain and I was called off the subs' bench to don the glad rags and hit the town to be fed interesting and imaginative food.

I admire the creativity and hard work of chefs whose food ticks all the boxes: tasty, different and lovely to look at. There are so many Irish chefs who are true artists and I was more than willing to sample the delights of one of them in Dublin on that Saturday evening. I was conscious of the fact that this was a step in the lead up to Mike and Anne's wedding eleven months later, and was pleased to be part of the celebration.

I prepared well for the night out. Got the hair done, chose a nice dress with a bit of wriggle room – I was going to be eating all round me, after all. I had eaten very little in anticipation of same and I was ready and waiting well in advance of the pick-up time. This was Mike and Anne's night and I didn't want to keep them waiting. I jumped into the back seat of the car beside Anita and we chatted about the feast that we were heading in to the city to devour. Mike said his dad had left his wallet at home and we were going to swing by the tennis club and drop it off to him. That was fine. We had to drive past the club anyway, so there would be no delay there. We three ladies sat in the car park chatting when Mike came out and said his dad would like us to go in for a drink before heading on to town. I was worried that we would be late for our booking and I didn't want Mike and Anne to be rushed or stressed. As I said earlier, this was their night. Or so I thought.

How wrong can a person be! There are still butterflies in my stomach as I recall the next few moments.

We went into the clubhouse, climbed the steps but instead of turning right to go to the bar, Mike and Anne turned left and seconds later the doors to the function room opened and I was propelled by a sharp dig in the back from Anita into this room packed with friends and family singing 'Happy Birthday' and 'Congratulations'. I was totally thrown, shocked beyond belief, overwhelmed. Actually, in this instance I think the word 'gobsmacked' fits the bill.

How did I respond to this amazing spectacle of smiling faces gathered there to celebrate my sixtieth birthday? True to form, I dissolved into a blubbering specimen, with tears flowing down my cheeks. So much for the careful make-up application for the night out with Anne and Mike! When the free-flowing tears had ebbed to a trickle, confusion set in. I was looking around at all of these people who had travelled from the four corners of the country, and some from abroad, and wondering what they would do when we had to leave for the wedding tasting in town. It took a few minutes for me to realise that there was no tasting and that this party was for me.

For the previous three months, Anita had spearheaded a committee, if you don't mind, to organise this surprise party in the tennis club (competition night, my eye) to mark my Big Six-O! And what a surprise it was. I had no inkling at any stage that this was going on behind my back.

My four children had been part of this select committee, even Lucy in Korea. I remember feeling a bit sorry for myself the week before this all happened because I had phoned from the car on my way home from a long day's filming for *Nationwide* and Eva, Tom and Eoin were in the house. I was looking forward to a cuppa and a chat but by the time I got home the house was empty. When they arrived back later, having 'gone for an ice-cream', I felt a bit put out that they hadn't waited until I had got home. I found out later a meeting had been called in the tennis club to make final decisions about decorating the party room.

Anita is an energetic, pragmatic and stylish organiser, full of ideas and willing to work hard to implement them. She could run a small country – now there's a thought! She and her committee met regularly in her house over the summer and everybody had their area of responsibility. I knew nothing about any of this. Such was the determination that I would not be suspicious that, as well as organising the wedding tasting for that evening, Anita was quite openly organising a dinner party in her house for two weeks later, the actual date of my birthday. The committee had ample opportunity to have their planning meetings, I suppose, because I was away a good bit for *Nationwide* that summer. They all enjoyed those meetings and missed the fun of the gatherings when the project was brought to a successful conclusion with that wonderful night in early September last year. Mission accomplished.

It was a spectacular and wonderful party. I enjoyed every minute of it when I'd got over the shock. It took a long time for me to absorb all of the elements that came together beautifully to make this memorable event. The room was bathed in soft pink and lilac lighting. They had hired a stage and a lighting rig. Life-size posters of yours truly were suspended from the ceiling, which were a bit scary to contemplate on entering the room. They were very nicely printed on shiny paper from photos that my brother had got from previous issues of the *RTÉ Guide*. I still have them upstairs. They could come in useful to place in front of the hearth to keep children away from the fire! Circular tables were covered with crisp white tablecloths and topped with tall vases, borrowed from Frank, the local florist, filled with delicate sprays of gypsophila. The room was festooned with white, pink and lilac helium balloons, some with a discreet 'Happy Birthday' on them, others with a full on 'Happy 60th'. Eoin and his girlfriend, Nicola, had collected them. Nicola is a very slim young woman and I'm surprised she managed to keep her feet on the ground and wasn't spotted airborne over the rooftops as she carried those masses of balloons from the car to the club.

A screen was showing photos on a loop. It had been Tom's job to organise those from family albums. I have loved taking photos since I was a child. In fact, some of my friends moan when we go anywhere because I like to capture the moment for posterity, which of course necessitates them standing where I tell them and smiling for the camera. Not much to ask, I think, but not everyone agrees! The chore of ironing is made pleasurable for me because I stand in the kitchen at the ironing board with a cup of tea on the side and my digital photo frame on shuffle in front of me. I reminisce about the happy times preserved in hundreds of photographs. I have joked with my children that I want them to have the photo frame playing at my funeral!

I was really pleased to see those photos at my sixtieth birthday party rather than having to wait till I have departed this life. I'd say my children are pleased too. They probably didn't relish the thought of telling a priest of my funeral request!

Michael, as well as playing a lot of tennis, also organises the social calendar of the tennis club and he is renowned for his barbecues and parties after tournaments. This was his area of responsibility on the night. He pulled out all the stops and ordered a pig to be roasted on a spit. Eva's boyfriend, Benny, and Eoin were afraid they'd have nightmares having been the ones tasked to carry the dead and very heavy pig from the delivery van to the roasting device on the balcony. The pork was accompanied by delicious salads and washed down with lovely prosecco in pretty glasses. The cake was a work of art. Michael's sister Kathleen is a great baker and she'd made a really apt cake – two cakes, in fact: a television set in the background and a woman standing in front of it with a microphone in her hand and a big smile on her face. Could that be me? Absolutely!

The telly was the old-fashioned roundy type; well, it was my sixtieth! It had a rabbit's ears on top, a throwback to the days of my childhood when we relied heavily on the antenna to get any type of picture. A reminder also of a funny moment in my broadcasting career a few years ago when I was MC at the televised launch of Saorview, the Irish free-to-air television service. I was onstage in Studio One in Montrose in front of an invited audience and when the red light came on and we were live to the nation I welcomed everyone to this moment that would improve the television service for so many Irish viewers in urban and rural locations. I reminisced about my early memories of black and white TV and the rabbit's ears that we had to tweak to the left or the right to get a picture. The studio audience, particularly those around my age, nodded and laughed at the memory. And then, as Gaeilge, I introduced the first of our speakers, the Minister for Communications, who at that time was ... Pat Rabbitte. Minister Rabbitte thanked me for my introduction, as Gaeilge, and then announced to the nation that I could tweak his ears anytime! The studio audience roared with laughter. I imagine the people viewing this momentous occasion, the launch of Saorview, howled in the comfort of their own homes. It was a gem and has been replayed on RTÉ comedy shows several times since.

Back to the tennis club and that amazing night that took me completely by surprise and got me thinking once again about what really matters in this life. No marks for guessing that it's all about people and relationships. I was very humbled that my family and friends had gone to so much trouble on my account.

I have to admit I felt a bit uncomfortable at the beginning, thinking to myself that they shouldn't have spent so much of their time and money organising this party for me. I'm fine. I don't need this celebration. They should look after themselves and not make a fuss of me. They very quickly pointed out to me that I like to do that kind of thing for others, which is true. I like to make a fuss of people and do special things for them. I do it because I want to. It's not a chore and I like the fact that it makes someone feel special. I certainly never want anything in return. I suppose this was the first time that I was conscious of the other side of giving, which is receiving.

I had never really thought about the reaction of others when they receive a kindness. That they might want to return the compliment and that we need to accept that graciously. The French writer Alexandre Dumas put it very clearly – and he should know a thing about friendship. He's the man who wrote *The Three Musketeers*, a title that has become part of the vernacular to describe a group of friends:

> *'Friendship consists in forgetting what one gives and remembering what one receives.'*

This surprise party was the moment for me to forget giving and enjoy receiving. As I say, I was deeply humbled and had a moment of awakening to what the people I know and love might think about me. It was a strange feeling and honestly not one that I had been conscious of before. I imagine there are a lot of people who are happy to do things for others without a thought as to how that doing and giving is valued. I hope that after reading about my awakening on that night they might sit back and look at what they do from the other person's perspective and accept, and indeed savour, the recognition. It's a nice moment of acceptance, acknowledging our worth, affirming generosity shown in the past and reminding us all that what matters is the people in our lives, how we treat them and also how they treat us.

When the penny had dropped and I realised I didn't have to apologise to the room full of people for having to leave them to go taste wedding food, I spent the evening going from table to table, chatting and laughing, hearing how my friends had been trying to avoid me in the previous few weeks for fear of letting the cat out of the bag.

Once again, I was humbled by the efforts people had made to be in the tennis club that night, that they would do this for me. I brushed off some of the very nice things that people said as we chatted. My generation was most definitely brought up to not think too highly of ourselves, to not get above ourselves. Praise was kept to a minimum for fear we'd get a big head. The result of that kind of upbringing is that it can be embarrassing to hear people sing our praises. That's a pity, really. We all benefit from a feeling of confidence yet we are conditioned by our upbringing to shut people down when they compliment us. As I reflected on the sea of positive emotions in that party room, I decided that I was going to continue to reach out to people in whatever way I could and that I was going to become a better receiver and allow people to reach out to me.

The party was a real family affair, and when I say family I mean blood relations and my family of dear friends. There's a fridge magnet that says our friends are the family we choose for ourselves. That's a good way of looking at the people in our lives. I am blessed with both types of family. My brother John was a very funny and very irreverent MC. No chance of a big head with John around. My brother Tony was official photographer, although he abdicated his responsibility later on and handed the camera to his daughters, my nieces Eimear and Ailbhe, who made a very good job of capturing people in candid moments! Deirdre started the singing and we had a very nice round of songs from guests who came up onstage and did a turn.

There were also the speeches – no point in having a stage if you don't have speeches. Eva, Tom and Eoin came up onstage and presented me with lovely flowers and big hugs and I cried again. I recovered my composure sufficiently to say a few words and marvel at the capacity of my friends to lie with such aplomb in the weeks leading up to this moment. I assured them that I would pray for the forgiveness of those lies in Lourdes, where I was heading the next day to film for *Nationwide* with the Dublin Diocesan Pilgrimage. I recounted my day of preparing for my night out with Anita, Mike and Anne. I had waved Eva, Tom and Eoin off at lunchtime. They were, allegedly, heading to Limerick for an overnight with Eva's boyfriend, who lives there. I had made cocktail sausages and fairy cakes and handed them into the car as they were leaving. The party committee in the tennis club laughed when the three arrived to the club five minutes later holding plates of sausages and buns. The club is only around the corner so they were still warm – and eaten with gusto!

The tears flowed again when I was asked to look to the big screen where the photos were suspended to make way for video messages organised by Eva. She had recorded pieces from Lucy in Korea and from John's daughter Clare in Perth. That was a difficult moment. I would have loved both of them to be there. And they were sorry to miss a family gathering. We tend to celebrate a lot in our family, so they knew what they were missing. It was a poignant moment for us all, watching them on screen so far away. I was conscious once again of the absolute heartbreak for families of emigrants who have left their homeplace out of necessity. Lucy and Clare both chose to travel to far-off places and they have had great adventures. My heart goes out to the emigrants who would much prefer to be at home and to their parents who would give their eye teeth to see them walk through the door.

Closer to home, Deirdre had recorded a video message from my godmother, Auntie Kathleen, Mam's last remaining sister, who had celebrated her ninetieth birthday the previous day. She was too frail to leave her home but all her nieces and nephews had gone to her house with flowers and a cake and we had had a little party there. I have to admire my cousins for their poker faces as we cut that cake and sang for Auntie Kathleen. They gave nothing away of the plans for my party.

Deirdre had also recorded a message from a neighbour of hers on Inis Mór, Bartla Winnie, a lovely old man who gives me rhubarb and potatoes from time to time. He spoke in Irish and everybody in the room fell in love with him instantly. It was quite a cosmopolitan video presentation, ranging from Korea to Australia to Dublin and the Aran Islands, that tugged at my heartstrings and made me feel very protective of my family and friends. At that moment, I felt I wanted to safeguard them all, at home and abroad. It's good to have reminders of how precious people are in our lives, how lucky we are to be surrounded by people who love us and who understand, support and accept us for who we are.

'Friendship improves happiness,
and abates misery by doubling our joys,
and dividing our grief.'
Cicero

The formalities gave way to a night of singing and dancing, from *céilí* to disco to moves that the younger generation manoeuvred their way through with ease and tried to teach to some of us elder lemons with very little success. There was a lot of Abba, a lot of air guitars and pretend microphones and an awful lot of fun. When our energies were spent with dancing, my nephew Dermot, an accomplished singer and guitarist, entertained us and a singsong began. I was unaware that the party actually continued with pizza, tea and more songs in Anita and Michael's house until the birds were singing and the day was dawning. Maybe it's just as well that I bypassed that after-party. I was, after all, heading to Lourdes the following day at lunchtime, where I did say prayers and light candles for all of the wonderful people who had taken the trouble to come to the party to help me celebrate that milestone birthday.

People often ask me how I feel about turning sixty. The answer is I feel grateful. I am conscious that, unless I live to be 120, I have lived more of my life than I have left to live. To be practical about the matter, my days are numbered. I have been very lucky in some aspects of my life. I had four healthy babies who are now healthy adults and good people. I have great friends from all walks of life. That party room last September was filled with friends from my childhood, from my days as a teacher, RTÉ friends, Rose of Tralee friends, people I met over the years on charity trips to Africa, others whom I got to know a few years ago when we formed a group to walk the Camino de Santiago, neighbours past and present, all dear friends. I have a job that I love which gives me the opportunity to indulge my passion for this country and my interest in my fellow countrymen and women.

I have also had sadness and setbacks in my life. I regret the breakdown of my marriage. I don't believe anybody walks up the aisle on their wedding day wanting anything other than their union to last for the rest of their lives. That doesn't always happen and the result is heartbreak, disruption, gut-wrenching sadness and a very difficult path to walk, negotiating the rearing of children and all the other aspects of life without the person you thought would be your partner for life.

I was twenty-one when my father died from a heart attack. I was teaching English in Brittany at the time and hadn't seen him in four months. That was my first introduction to the heart-rending grief of losing a loved one. I remember wanting to take a fold-up chair and sit by his grave on the night of his funeral. I couldn't bear the thought of his body lying in the cold, dark earth of the graveyard. I just wanted to hold him. I also remember returning to Brittany after the funeral to find a letter that he had written to me a couple of days before he'd died. As you can imagine, it is one of my most treasured possessions. Since then, there have been other sad losses, including the death of my mother, which I have written about and which has opened up so many conversations with people I've met who have also lost their mothers. It's a comfort to know we all face similar challenges in life. We are not alone. Life is a mixture of happy and sad times. We need one to recognise the other.

As I embark on this new decade. I am determined to enjoy life as fully as I can. Like I said, my days are numbered. I want to savour the moments. A highlight of the summer was a delightfully quiet weekend in the west with my daughter Eva. We went for walks, drank coffee, watched TV on our beds in our bathrobes, had a massage and chatted and laughed a lot. I realise these are precious moments. They must be savoured. Who knows what's around the corner for any of us.

I have resolved to be less hard on myself and allow myself to just be. I have a tendency to be always on the go. In fairness, a certain amount of that is due to the travel involved with *Nationwide*, although even when I'm not travelling for work, I tend to be rushing about a lot. I have to train myself to enjoy the solitude of being alone and to avoid the temptation to organise something in case I'll feel lonely and sad. I realise that I will have lonely moments and dark days. They too are part of this stage of life and cannot be avoided but I hope they can be tolerated through the realisation that the darkness will cede to light and that tomorrow is another day.

My aspirations are simple for this new decade and they revolve around people: family, friends and perhaps new friends whom I will meet along the way. I have got to a stage where I cannot summon up much enthusiasm about material possessions anymore. I am happy in my house but I am not eager to buy little bits and pieces for it in the same way I was in years gone by. Some might say that's because the house has everything that's needed. I don't think so. There are always things to buy, styles to change. I just don't have the enthusiasm for that anymore.

I enjoy my home and I love my garden but what makes them really special for me is the opportunity they provide for people to spend time here, to relax, to chat, to have fun. I wonder is this something that comes with the advent of the Big Six-O. It has for me anyway. I actually enjoy giving things away to friends if they admire something I have. It gives me pleasure to see them having a use for something I have owned. I'm not alone in this newly acquired habit. I remember being deeply moved hearing the story of Fr Mychal Judge, the chaplain to the New York Fire Department who was the first certified fatality of the attacks on the Twin Towers in 2001. The image of his body being carried by firefighters from the North Tower on a chair covered in dust has been described as an American Pietà. Three thousand people attended his funeral in St Francis of Assisi Church in Manhattan and when it was time to empty out his humble cell in the Franciscan monastery attached to the church, people were surprised to find it almost bare. Fr Mychal had given away most of his worldly possessions, his books, his clothes, his music. He did have a reputation for passing on valuables to those in need. Steven McDonald, a retired detective with NYPD, writing in the *New York Times* said of him after he died:

'Mychal had no use for physical things. Give him a cashmere sweater and it would end up on the back of a homeless person. But go to him with a troubled soul and he would listen intently for as long as it took.'

Fr Mychal was a man who valued human interaction much more than any worldly goods but to have given away almost everything was remarkable. He was a man who understood the difficulties that life can present. He was an alcoholic who achieved sobriety in 1978 after spending eight years in Alcoholics Anonymous. His sexual orientation was gay, although he lived the life of a celibate priest. He was a much-loved figure on the streets of Manhattan, ministering to the down and outs, the homeless, the drug addicts, and he loved his work as chaplain to the New York Fire Department. I have huge admiration for Fr Mychal Judge, as a person and as a pastor.

Like most people, I was touched by the image of this man, his head slumped to one side, covered in dust, being carried on a chair by the men he cared for in the fire department. It was only after 9/11 that I realised he was the son of Irish immigrants from County Leitrim and in the tiny village of Keshcarrigan, there is a lovely peace garden, which was built in his memory in 2005 on land that was once owned by his ancestors.

Fr Mychal was born in Brooklyn, a twin, although his sister Dympna was born two days after him. His father died when he was six and to help his mother, he used to shine shoes outside Penn Station, across the road from the church of St Francis of Assisi. He was captivated by the sight of the Franciscans coming and going in the area, 'I knew then that I wanted to be a friar.' He certainly followed in the footsteps of St Francis, walking the streets of New York, holding people close in his arms as they died of AIDS, giving them comfort and blessings. He was a great man for blessing people at the end of a conversation in the street.

There are those who regard Fr Mychal as a saint. We may never have heard of him in Ireland, I suppose, if he had continued in his ministry untouched by the tragedy of 9/11. He didn't hesitate when the North Tower was hit and went in to the lobby to pray over the rescuers, the dead and the wounded. Then, when the South Tower collapsed, debris flew into the lobby of the North Tower and he was killed, certified as Victim 0001, the first casualty to be brought out from the wreckage.

I feel proud of Fr Mychal Judge. He showed us that what matters in life is kindness, compassion and love. Materialistic concerns were obviously very far from his mind. I'm delighted that he is celebrated in Keshcarrigan, the village of his ancestors, with a stone bench surrounded by gravel and flowers and looking out over the lake. A tranquil, peaceful setting for a man of peace and love.

Back to sixty-year-old me and the path stretching ahead of me as I enter a new decade. Wow. What will I be like at seventy? How can I even mention the word? There are people who are surprised at me for admitting that I am sixty even. Why not? It's life. It's progress. There is no age I have been to which I would like to return. I am the accumulation of all of the ages that I have lived. I have been influenced by my upbringing, by my education, by travel, by challenge, by good and bad fortune. And this is me. I aspire to spending lots of time with my family and my friends, celebrating life in the way my life was celebrated by that wonderful surprise party last September.

There were other gatherings to mark the milestone. In fact, the year has been a series of celebrations, from weekends away to concerts and other outings, and as recently as last month, a dear friend produced a birthday cake while three of us were having dinner in her house in Cork. I'll miss all the fuss when I turn sixty-one! I will, however, never forget the message the year has made ever clearer to me, that people and love are what matter, that no man is an island: we are all in this together.

'Friendship is born at that moment
when one person says to another:
"What! You too? I thought I was the only one."'
C. S. Lewis

'Happy marriages begin when we marry the ones we love, and they blossom when we love the ones we marry.'

Tom Mullen

10.

Love is in the Air

'A thing of beauty is a joy forever:
Its loveliness increases; it will never
Pass into nothingness; but still will keep
A bower quiet for us, and a sleep
Full of sweet dreams, and health, and
quiet breathing.'
John Keats

Those opening lines from John Keats' long poem *Endymion* are beautiful and perfect for the mood in our family right now. The poem is based on the story from Greek mythology about the shepherd Endymion who was loved by the moon goddess Selene. She visited him at night-time – obviously, she being the moon goddesss! She asked Zeus to grant Endymion eternal life. I'm not sure how successful that request was but Keats has certainly touched on some very important aspects of life and love: the peace of quiet breathing, the joy of good health and sweet dreams, and the loveliness of caring for somebody and wanting to look after them.

If a highlight of last year was my sixtieth birthday and the good wishes of true friends, then the highlight for this year is undoubtedly the engagement of my daughter Eva and her boyfriend, now fiancé, Benny. I've mentioned them a few times already (they were part of the organising committee for my surprise party in the tennis club). It is my pleasure now to pull out all the stops and celebrate their wonderful news. Theirs will be the first wedding in either family, and we are all excited and delighted for them both.

Eva and Benny spent a fun, action-packed holiday in the States and Canada last summer. They hired a car in JFK and drove to Washington for a few days, followed by a few more at a lake house in Syracuse. Then, it was on to

Canada via Niagra Falls, an interesting time sightseeing in Toronto and an overnight in a winery on the way back to New York, New York, so good they named it twice.

It was in the city that never sleeps that Benny proposed to my eldest child, and there are locations in Ireland that never slept that night such was the excitement after the phone call came from the US around seven in the evening their time, midnight for us. A bit late perhaps to be phoning friends and relations to tell them the good news? Not at all. The phones were hopping. Those friends and relations who were woken from their slumber were delighted to be part of the happy event.

I had just finished filming traditional music and set-dancing in a pub in west Clare for a *Nationwide* programme about Marty Morrissey when Eva phoned. We had enjoyed a great night of music and camaraderie, and Marty telling everybody the news of the engagement brought the evening to a very happy conclusion. Benny, a Limerick man, was delighted to hear that Marty had announced his engagement to Eva in Quilty. He's a big fan of the GAA commentator from the Banner county. I was really looking forward to giving Eva and Benny a big hug, but that had to wait until they returned four days later, by which time I had left for Kerry to chair the judging panel for the 2015 International Rose of Tralee. However, there was no way I was going to have them return to my empty house without some bit of celebratory feel to the occasion. What does a decoration fan do in a situation like that? Well, this one bought banners, glitter, petals and paper chains. That may sound like the Queen of Tack was losing the run of herself but, believe me, it was all very tasteful, subtle and understated. The glitter was silver and heart-shaped, the paper chains were white and in the shape of doves and wedding bells, and the banners were banners!

When they arrived back to Dublin, tired and jetlagged at the end of their overnight flight, and opened the kitchen door, they got a peek at what the following weeks and months would bring. The table was covered in a crisp white damask cloth, scattered with glitter and petals, small gifts and cards and with white doves and bells looking down on it. The atmosphere was of celebration and congratulations. I hope it was a nice moment on their own in the kitchen, realising that friends and family were delighted for them and wanted to wish them well.

'Marriage is a promise.
Not just between the couple but to the
community at large, to generations past
and to those yet to be born.'

Anon.

There was a wonderful sense of community around Eva and Benny's engagement. After a few hours' rest, they drove down to Tralee to share their good news with brothers, cousins, aunts and uncles who had decamped there for the festival – which is always a wonderful occasion, well loved and supported by my family. We were all looking forward to seeing them and they us. What they didn't know was that the festival organisers, when they realised they were coming to Tralee, organised a little party for them in my room. When they knocked on the door of Room 104 in the Fels Point Hotel, they had no idea that on the other side was a gathering of about twenty people. They were expecting the family to be there, but were certainly not expecting my four fellow judges, former judges and former Roses, the head of tourism with Kerry County Council, several members of the Rose of Tralee organising committee and Benny's best friend Ray and his new wife Helen, a Tralee woman who happened to be home for the festival. Benny had been best man at their wedding a mere six weeks previously. You know what they say about going to a wedding being the making of another!

The look on Benny and Eva's faces as they absorbed the group of people in the room was a sight to behold. They were totally surprised, a bit shy at first but delighted that so many people wanted to share in their moment. They were humbled by the efforts the hotel had gone to on their behalf. Eva had accompanied me to the Rose of Tralee on a number of occasions, and the festival family wanted to congratulate her and Benny.

The room was decorated with nightlights and little glass vases with red roses floating in water. There were red paper rose petals strewn around the table, canapés to pass around, champagne flutes with a strawberry stuck in the rim and an ice bucket with bottles of prosecco. There was a bouquet of flowers, roses of course, and a lovely feeling of celebration and support in the room.

The community at large was ready and willing to share the good news of this engagement. The Rose of Tralee family was there to welcome and embrace Eva and Benny. I felt very honoured that these people, whom I have got to know over the eight years during which I have judged the International Rose, took the time and the trouble to make a fuss of my daughter and her fiancé in the middle of a hectic few days in Tralee. Such people-centred moments are definitely part of the important things in life. We all chatted and toasted and then dispersed, some returning to their duties, others preparing to meet their families and our gang went off to Fenit for dinner and lots of wedding talk.

Eva and Benny had been together for eighteen months at the time of their engagement. They had met in Limerick just as Eva was coming to the end of her post-graduate course in Mary Immaculate College to become a primary-school teacher. She had taken the brave step of resigning from her permanent job in the bank to become a student again at the age of twenty-nine in order to fulfil her dream of being a teacher. That dream brought her to 'Mary I' in Limerick, and there she met Benny. The timing was perfect really. He was able to help Eva with all the cutting and pasting and laminating for her teaching practice. Anyone who has been through teaching practice will understand the amount of work involved and the fact that this fledgling relationship survived it, with all its long hours of preparation, augured well for the future.

Benny is a gentle, patient man and from the time he was introduced to the family when the exams were over and the summer holidays had begun, he has been a very easy guest in all situations. His introduction was a baptism of fire really. He happened to come to Dublin the weekend of a family barbecue so he was thrown in at the deep end and met everyone belonging to Eva all in one go. Not for the faint hearted! But he stayed, settled in and joined in the fun.

'The bond that links your true family is not one of blood, but of respect and joy in each other's life.'

Those are the words of the writer and aviator Richard Bach, author of the seventies' bestseller *Jonathan Livingston Seagull* and they definitely apply to my family.

We lead busy lives but we have no problem taking time out to party, have fun and share in each other's joys. Benny didn't seem overwhelmed by his introduction to the whole family in one go. Just as well because there will be lots of parties and celebrations as we embark on a year of wedding preparations. I can hardly wait.

It's a lovely feeling to see your daughter or son happy in a relationship, and I don't take for granted the fact that Eva has become engaged to a kind, decent, gentle man. They are good together. He will be a good husband to her and she will be a good wife to him. They are conscious of each other's needs and I know that each of them wants to make the other happy. That is a blessing.

'Success in marriage does not come merely through finding the right mate, but through being the right mate.'
Barnett R. Brickner

WHAT MATTERS

Everybody who knows Eva and Benny sees they are perfect for each other. His mother Mary is as delighted to be welcoming Eva into their family as I am to have Benny in ours. There's a busy year ahead. Eva will be teaching in Dublin for the year and studying for her professional teaching diploma. Benny will be working in Limerick and we will all be planning a wedding. Happy days ahead and it couldn't happen to two nicer, more well-grounded people. As Antoine de Saint-Exupéry, a man of great wisdom and insight, said:

'Love does not consist of gazing at each other, but in looking together in the same direction.'

That's Eva and Benny. Go raibh saol fada, sona acu le chéile.

'Things do not change, we change.'

Henry David Thoreau

11.

Field of Dreams

'Out beyond ideas of wrongdoing
and right doing there is a field.
I'll meet you there.
When the soul lies down in that grass
the world is too full to talk about.'

Rumi

Isn't that a lovely thought, that there is a place we can go to where we are free of talk of what's right and what's wrong, of expectations and responsibilities, of concerns and worries, a grassy glade, perhaps, where we can leave the concerns of daily life to one side and get in touch with the soul, with who we are and what we are: thinking, feeling, caring, loving beings. Easier said than done, I know, but increasingly important, I think, as life gets more and more demanding.

At certain stages, that demand manifests itself in terms of working long hours to carve out a career, of racing hither and thither rearing children and then, when they are reared and have flown the nest, that life demand can manifest itself in terms of coping with loneliness and sadness. One of the important life lessons that I have garnered in recent years is that I am responsible for my own happiness, that I must look inside myself to find contentment, that nobody else can truly make me happy. As you would expect, Rumi has hit the nail on the head in this area of the human condition.

> 'Do you know what you are?
> You are a manuscript of a divine letter.
> You are a mirror reflecting a noble face.
> The universe is not outside of you.
> Look inside yourself;
> Everything that you want,
> you are already that.'

You will have gleaned from reading some of the previous chapters of this book that I am not immune to loneliness and dark days. My coping strategy has always been to keep busy, to be on the go the whole time. I am lucky to have deep reserves of energy so it's no hardship for me to get into the car at six in the morning and drive long distances to film for a day and then to drive back home. I tell myself that I like to sleep in my own bed. That is true but I also want to be ready to get going the following day as well – sometimes it's work, sometimes it's leisure.

There are many examples of this particular idiosyncrasy; one that springs to mind happened last year. I celebrated Mother's Day in style with three women friends in Paris. We had a wonderful time, sightseeing, shopping, wining, dining and talking for Ireland. It was therapeutic, fun and pretty hectic, and on Sunday evening four tired bunnies made their way to the airport. My three friends travelled home to Ireland. I, on the other hand, headed off to Mozambique to film for five days for a *Nationwide* programme about the work of Irish ophthalmologists who provide eye care in remote parts of that country. It was exhausting but I wouldn't have missed Paris or Mozambique for the world.

Another example of that busyness is flying to Lourdes for a week the morning after my sixtieth birthday party. I take no responsibility for that schedule, though. After all, I thought I was spending the eve of that trip quietly tasting a wedding menu!

I know I have a huge appetite for adventure and for making the most of all opportunities. I enjoy challenges and overcoming obstacles, learning new skills, meeting new people. In recent years, I have become an active member of a local charity, following in my father's footsteps. He had been a founder member of the group many years ago in Clondalkin. At the beginning of this year, I joined a local choir, something I have wanted to do for a long time. It matters to me that these two activities are local. They give me a sense of belonging to my community and that is a very comforting feeling. I see the huge benefits of community as I travel the country for *Nationwide*, the difference organisations like Tidy Towns make to a place and, more particularly, to the people living in that place.

I also know, though, that it's important for all of us to have down time, to do as Rumi says and search for that field where the world will not encroach on us, to look inside ourselves, to explore the universe that is not outside of us. My default position has tended to be activity always. I think, in a way, I have been frightened of standing still, of looking inside myself. I have been staving off the risk of loneliness by maintaining a hectic pace. The truth of the matter is that loneliness and sadness find us where we are and failure to acknowledge them does not make them go away. Deep down, I know this and I have put a lot of energy into slowing down, not looking for escape, living in the present moment. Sr Stan, a woman I admire greatly and have already written about, is a great advocate of mindfulness, of living in the now and allowing instinct and intuition to lead us to an honest response to the good things and the bad things that life puts in our path.

'Life is a series of natural and
spontaneous changes.
Don't resist them – that only creates sorrow.
Let reality be reality.
Let things flow naturally forward in
whatever way they like.'
Lao Tzu

Excellent advice there from the ancient Chinese philosopher and poet that would see us embrace wholly the joys and sorrows of this life.

I look on life as a sacred journey. I have a loving family, and loyal and true friends. These form the cornerstones of my life. I am also privileged to have met really inspirational people along the way. I have written about some of them already. They share compassion, love and caring as the mainstays of their personalities; also, most importantly, a sense of humour and fun.

Debbie Deegan ticks all of those boxes. She is the woman who founded the charity To Russia with Love in 1988 following a trip to a remote orphanage, an overnight train ride from Moscow, from where she adopted a seven-year-old girl to join her husband and two young children in Dublin. Debbie had promised this young girl that she would visit the children with whom she had spent the first seven years of her life. But she was ill prepared for the horror of what she found there: children living in filthy grey institutional buildings in freezing conditions due to broken windows. What struck her most was the lack of love shown to these children. She let her heart rule her head and took the orphanage under her wing.

I visited that orphanage a few years ago and those grey soulless buildings had been replaced by small brightly coloured bungalows, one of the first improvements Debbie undertook. She invited the children to choose the colours for their new homes and the resultant palette of pink, yellow, purple and blue is an indication of the brightness that she has brought into their lives.

Russian orphans are not necessarily without parents. Many of them come from homes where alcoholism and drug addiction have rendered their parents incapable of caring for them. Most children are taken into pretty grim state-run institutions. The lucky ones end up in Debbie's care. The children ran down the driveway to welcome Debbie the day I visited with her, and they were full of energy and smiles. All except one pale little boy with a sore on his lip and matted hair who had only arrived that day and found it hard to comprehend the fun and laughter all around him. I have no doubt he is now one of the gang and thriving in an environment of love and care.

WHAT MATTERS

To Russia with Love provides hope for the future to so many abandoned children. At eighteen years of age, the young people leave the orphanage and live in small groups with a house parent in an apartment owned by the charity, well on their way to independent living and a good life. Debbie numbers doctors, teachers, lawyers, mechanics and accountants among her 'children', as she calls them. They all remain fiercely loyal to this Irishwoman and the orphanage that gave them a chance in life.

What a difference this one woman has made. What an inspiring role model for us in this fast-paced world where so often the emphasis is on doing and acquiring. She is the epitome of compassion and love, and has a fighting spirit that sees her taking on any challenge to help others, a woman whose life's work reminds us every day of what truly matters: people, our nearest and dearest, those whose lives we touch from time to time, and ourselves. Lao Tzu had his finger on the pulse of what is important in life and his words have a real resonance even now, more than 2,000 years after he wrote them. I began this chapter with Rumi's lovely image of a field of dreams and I'd like to finish with this uplifting affirmation of, quite simply, what matters.

'Simplicity, patience, compassion.
These three are your greatest treasures.
Simple in actions and thoughts, you return to the
source of being. Patient with both friends and
enemies, you accord with the way things are.
Compassionate toward yourself,
you reconcile all beings in the world.'

Lao Tzu